THE ZILLI
FISH COOKBOOK

ALDO ZILLI

THE ZILLI FISH COOKBOOK

QUICK AND EASY RECIPES
FROM BRITAIN'S TOP FISH RESTAURANT

Published by Metro Publishing Ltd,
3 Bramber Court, 2 Bramber Road, London W14 9PB, England

First published in hardback in 2002

ISBN 1 84358 022 5

British Library Cataloguing-in-Publication Data: A catalogue record for this
book is available from the British Library.

Edited by Arlene Sobel
Designed by Alison Shackleton
Food photography by Gus Filgate
Stylist Susie Theodorou
Jacket design by ENVY
Typeset by Wakewing, High Wycombe, Buckinghamshire

Plates and dishes used in the photogrpahs on pages 39 and 123:
Friache Collection, Poole Pottery.
Indian Stone bowls and platters used in the
photographs on pages 43, 59, 74, 143, 115:
David Wainwright (020 8960 8181)

Printed and bound in Italy by Eurolitho S.p.A., Milan

1 3 5 7 9 10 8 6 4 2

Papers used by Metro Publishing Ltd are natural, recyclable products made from
wood grown in sustainable forests. The manufacturing processes conform to the
environmental regulations of the country of origin.

CONTENTS

Acknowledgements

Zilli Fish restaurant has been a great inspiration for this book and all the recipes. I would like to thank my personal assistant Luisa Alves for all the hard work she puts in when I am writing books and for understanding my scribbles.

I would also like to thank my chefs Enzo di Marino and Toto Siragusa for putting up with my mood swings, and the Manager Gino Tozzi for keeping the service going while I take time out to write.

A very special thanks to my gorgeous daughter Laura for helping in the office while Luisa helps me.

To Susie Theodorou, my food stylist and home economist. She knows me so well now and made the food look exactly how I imagined it would in the photos.

A special thanks to Poole Pottery for providing such wonderful dishes for the photoshoot and, in particular, Kirk Hoatson. He found the perfect location for the seaside picture of me, and didn't complain about the freezing cold weather that day, despite of being left stranded waiting for transport! Also, thank you to Adrian Houston, represented by White Ink, for taking some great shots on that photoshoot and for being extremely patient. Thanks to Alonzo for the many early morning starts we had in the office, and to me – for choosing such a wonderful team!

As always I would like to extend a big thank you to all my chefs, managers and staff for keeping the restaurants and office running smoothly, and to Gus Filgate for his fantastic food photography. Also to my publishers, my agent Fiona Lindsay, Antonio Alfano from Ciborio and to Delverde for supplying the pasta and olive oils for the recipes.

Introduction

As a child, money was always tight in my family. So to help during the school holidays I worked with the local fisherman, doing odd jobs such as carrying buckets of sea water back to the shop to keep the fish fresh. No school child ever got paid cash – instead we were given fish to take home for supper. This is how I became acquainted with fish from an early age. The knowledge came from my mother, who I used to help cook the catch of the day, and who allowed me to experiment. In my home town of Alba Adriatica all the restaurants served fish – it was practically all you could eat, and that also helped me develop a passion for eating fish and seafood.

My first real jobs were working in the hotels and restaurants in the fishing village where, naturally, they were very skilled at preparing fish – another learning experience. When I moved to England 22 years ago I again started experimenting with different foods and cooking methods, but my love of fish continued.

Zilli Fish was like a dream come true – I had always wanted to open a seafood restaurant. When I arrived here I was surprised to find so few fish restaurants, but since then people's tastes have changed dramatically. However, it was only in 1997 that I felt confident enough to open a restaurant dedicated exclusively to fish.

My aim in this book is to give you the chance to recreate some of my very early recipes such as the family roasts and the Traditional Italian Fish Stew, then gradually bring you up to date with recipes from Zilli Fish, such as Thai Mixed Seafood and Vegetable Brochettes and Tuna Escalope with Parma Ham and Sage. These dishes and others in the repertoire have been drawing the crowds since the restaurant opened. It's good to see so many other restaurants following suit. Now every good restaurant has seafood on its menu!

I love the range of textures, flavours and colours of seafood dishes – they can look quite dramatic and exciting. Today fish is less of a luxury and more of an everyday item. And with people becoming more health conscious they are automatically turning to fish.

The recipes here are made for experimenting – you can easily adjust them by changing the fish or other ingredients to suit your palate or the ingredients you have on hand. Remember, simplicity and enjoyment are the key elements and they will give you the chance to be creative. Fish is good for you and it tastes delicious. I hope you enjoy these recipes and that they encourage you to eat fish more often.

Fish Made Easy

It's so amazing to find how many people say, 'Oh, I don't like fish', when all they mean is that they don't know how to cook it or it seems too fiddly to eat. Here are 10 good reasons why more people should eat fish:

1 Eating fish is good for you. People who eat a lot of fish tend to live longer, as demonstrated by the Japanese who love fish. The National Health Foundation recommends that you should eat oily fish twice a week and white fish once a week as part of a balanced diet.

2 People who eat fish regularly, particularly oily fish such as mackerel and herring, have less risk of heart disease because it helps lower cholesterol in the blood. Fish is also rich in vitamins and minerals.

3 Preparing fish is simplicity itself once you know how to do it (I'll tell you in the next few pages). Don't be put off by the skin and bones as they can be dealt with by your fishmonger.

4 Fish that is cooked properly – that is until it's tender, not dry and overcooked – is a joy to eat. Whenever possible, serve the fish immediately after cooking so it that it will remain moist.

5 Remember that fish is extremely versatile: it makes wonderful soups and chowders, is perfect in salads and for barbecues, as a main course, served with pasta and rice, used in a curry or quiche or simply by itself.

6 Fish is extremely quick to cook – just take a look at the cooking times in my recipes. Once you discover this for yourself you'll be a fish eater for the rest of your life.

7 Fresh fish in season is fabulous because it's at its best. If you eat frozen fish, do so within two months of it being caught. Canned fish, while very different to fresh, has a longer shelf life and makes a good storecupboard standby.

8 Because each type of fish lends itself to different cooking methods – from poaching to grilling to roasting, to name just a few – you'll never be at a loss to produce new and different meals. Use the correct cooking method and you'll be sure to get wonderful results.

9 Fish is very nutritious. It's an excellent source of protein, many types are low in fat and, when plainly cooked, it's low in calories.

10 Fish and seafood, when it is cooked and presented properly, can look truly fantastic – give it a go to really impress your friends and family. Overcome your fears and inhibitions and lack of knowledge – fish will reward you every time.

Expert help

Find yourself a good fishmonger, the busier the better, because it means that they have a bigger turnover of fish and it will be much fresher. The local fishmonger enjoys working with fish and loves nothing more than chatting about what's best in that day and the ideal way to cook it. Remember that it's also part of the fishmonger's service to clean, gut, scale and fillet the fish. If you ask, they'll hand over the bones so you can make a good Fish Stock at home (see page 164 for my recipe). The fishmonger will cook lobsters and crabs for you on the premises and then clean any bits that need to be cleaned; they'll also clean scallops and squid (but not mussels or prawns). Some fishmongers will also smoke fish such as cod and haddock.

Choosing fresh fish

When buying fish, your senses of sight, smell and even touch are very important. Fresh fish should not smell 'fishy'; any that have a strong fishy ammonia smell are to be avoided. The fish should have clear eyes that are not sunken or dull. The gills should be bright red and not greying. The tail should be easy to bend and not dry, and the flesh of the fish should be quite firm – if you can bend the tail right over to the head, then do not buy this fish. Also, if you gently press the fish, the flesh should spring back when you lift your finger. Slime on fish needs to be clear – if opaque, then the fish is stale. Scaly fish such as salmon, sea bass, red mullet and snapper should have a good covering of scales – if they're falling off then this indicates that the fish is not at its best.

When choosing shellfish, you'll be looking for different qualities, except for the smell, which should be the same as when buying fish. The shells on shellfish must be tight and uncracked, and in the case of mussels and clams, the shells must close when you tap them on a hard surface; if they don't, avoid them. If you are buying live lobsters, the tail should spring back under the body when they are picked up, and also the legs should wriggle around (the same applies to live crabs); you should also avoid any with frothy mouths. Lobsters and crabs should feel heavy when handled. When you are buying cooked lobsters, the tail should be curled tightly into its body; if it's straight, it's most likely to have been cooked when dead and should therefore be avoided. Squid should have a clear white body with no tinge of red.

Not all fish are available fresh year-round, so check with your fishmonger, who may be able to supply the frozen variety.

Types of fish

I won't describe the fish individually here as each recipe has an introduction that explains its qualities and how it should be cooked. But, generally, fish and shellfish fall into the following categories:

WHITE FISH

FLAT FISH: This group includes Dover sole, halibut, lemon sole, plaice, skate and turbot.

ROUND FISH: Here we have bream, cod, coley, eel, haddock, hake, John Dory, monkfish, red mullet and sea bass.

OILY FISH

This healthful group of fish includes anchovies, herring, mackerel, pilchards, sardines, tuna and whitebait.

SHELLFISH

CRUSTACEANS: These are the ones with legs, and include crabs, langoustines (scampi), lobsters, prawns and shrimps.

MOLLUSCS: These legless fish are clams, mussels, oysters, scallops and winkles and the cephalopods cuttlefish, octopus and squid.

EXOTICS

As their names suggests! These include snapper and swordfish.

To this list we can add the ever-popular farmed fish such as salmon (which also comes wild) and trout.

I should also mention that many fish can be smoked – mackerel, salmon and trout – and also salted, like cod. See my recipes for more details.

White fish are sold in a range of different cuts, including fillets, cutlets, steaks and, in the case of round fish, middle cut; they are also, of course, sold whole.

Storing fish

Ideally fish should be cooked as soon as it's bought if it's to be enjoyed at its best, but it needs to be stored correctly beforehand.

After you've purchased fresh fish you should unwrap it and make sure that it has been gutted and gilled; otherwise do it now (see below). Ensure the cavity is clean and dry (even if the fishmonger did the cleaning for you). Transfer the fish to a plate large enough to hold the whole fish. Cover loosely with cling film and chill in the coldest part of the fridge. Check every 24 hours: if there are any juices replace the plate with a clean one and change the cling film every 24 hours.

If possible, keep whole fish on the bone, but it should be gutted and gilled; ensure that the cavity is clean and dry. Treat fish fillets, steaks and cutlets in the same way and use within 48 hours.

Live shellfish should be stored in a clean salad drawer in the fridge (with no salad in it as it will absorb the smells), covered with a damp tea towel. Oysters need to be stored in the same way but upside down so that they stay moist. Lobsters and crabs can be kept alive in the cool part of the fridge, covered with a damp tea towel (see page 11 for chilling lobster before it's cooked).

FREEZING

Fish should not be frozen for more than two months as it deteriorates. Thawed frozen fish must never be re-frozen, so check with the fishmonger that the fish is fresh. When freezing fish at home, be sure that the fish is clean, pat it dry with kitchen paper and wrap it well in cling film and then a freezer bag.

Preparing fish

Don't forget your fishmonger will do lots of the preparation for you. However if you want or need to do any of the preparation yourself, it's easier than you might imagine; all you need is a good sharp filleting knife and chopping board.

SCALING

Fish that need to be scaled include red mullet, salmon and sea bass. Draw the back of a strong knife (or scaling knife) along the fish from the tail to the head. This can be quite messy so place plenty of newspaper around the fish or work in the sink.

GUTTING

This is something the fishmonger never fails to do. But, just in case it hasn't been done already, make a slit along the base of the fish, starting below the head, and cut through to the soft part of the belly. Pull out the innards and blood line which runs along the bone with the innards. Wash the fish under cold running water. Using scissors, carefully cut away the gills and fins, if liked.

FILLETING FLAT FISH

Flat fish are filleted into two or four half pieces. Place the fish on a chopping board with the tail towards you. Cut through the flesh into the backbone, then along the length of the fish, then slide the filleting knife under the left fillet and cut close to the bones to remove the fillet. Turn the fish around so the head faces towards you and repeat to remove the right fillet. Turn the fish over and repeat to remove the other two fillets.

FILLETING ROUND FISH

A round fish will yield two fillets. Place the fish on a chopping board. Holding it taut on the board with one hand, cut through the flesh down to the backbone from the head to the tail. Insert the filleting knife between the flesh and the bones, and slice the fillet away from the bones, working in short strokes. Keep the knife as close to the bones as possible.

PIN-BONING

This process is necessary to remove the tiny bones that remain after filleting. Place the fillet flat on a chopping board, skin-side down, and run your fingers along the flesh to feel for any bones; pull the bones out using a pair of tweezers.

BUTTERFLY METHOD OF BONING

Small fish such as herrings, mackerels, red mullet and sardines can be completely boned with the two fillets kept intact at the top, making them perfect for stuffing and less tricky to eat. (See page 38 for butterflying prawns.)

Split the cleaned fish open, completely cutting along the length of the belly. Open out the fish, skin-side up, on a chopping board. Using the ball of your hand, press along the backbone of the fish, flat on the board. Turn the fish over, skin-side down, cut through the bone close to the head, and pull it out with all, or nearly all, the side bones attached to it. Pin-bone the remaining bones.

SKINNING FILLETS

You do not have to skin all the fish: the skin adds good flavour and, also, extra crispness when roasting, grilling and pan-frying.

To skin fillets before cooking, place the fillet on a chopping board, skin-side down, with the tail end towards you. Using a thin-bladed filleting knife, separate a little skin from the flesh at the tail. Sprinkle a little salt on this small piece of separated skin – this will help you grip the skin with two fingers. Slide the knife between the flesh and skin and push the knife away from you in a gentle sawing action to remove the skin in one piece.

In some instances, the fish can be skinned after cooking. Normally this is when the fish is poached or boiled – simply pull the skin off.

Preparing shellfish

LOBSTER: You can order cooked lobsters from your local fishmonger and they'll cook them on the day required. The are two methods that you can use to cook lobster at home.

The most humane method of cooking live lobsters is to first put them into a freezer to make them sleepy (a cool box in the fridge is not good enough).

For boiling, bring a Court Bouillon (see page 165) in a large deep pan to the boil and simmer for 30 minutes. Weigh the lobster then put in the court bouillon. Return to the boil, cover, reduce the heat and simmer for 10 minutes per 450g (1lb); the lobster will turn bright red. Using tongs, lift the lobster out and allow to cool before splitting. Halve the lobster lengthways and remove the stomach sac and thread-like intestine to serve. This method of cooking is best for lobster that is to be used cold, in salads or in dishes served with a light sauce. When boiling lobsters they tend to curl, but if you want the lobster to remain straight, you can tie the body to a small piece of wood that is the same length as the body (head to tail and not including the claws).

The second way of cooking lobster is to place the well-chilled lobster on a chopping board. Using the point of a sharp heavy knife, stab through the lobster's nerve centre which is located at the base of the head where it joins the body – it will die instantaneously. Then halve the lobster lengthways, open it out and remove the stomach sac and the thread-like intestine. The lobster can now be barbecued, grilled or chargrilled. If you do not want to deal with a live lobster at any stage, you can still grill and barbecue a boiled lobster (see page 14 for grilling and barbecuing).

PRAWNS AND LANGOUSTINES: Small crustaceans only need to be submerged in boiling Court Bouillon (see page 165), covered and boiled for 3–4 minutes until they turn bright pink. Prawns and langoustines can also be pan-fried, grilled or barbecued without being boiled first. Large prawns often have a large black vein (intestine) that runs along the outside curve. Peel the prawn and then, using a sharp knife, make a small incision along the length of the back and carefully pull out the black vein. If the shells are to be kept on, use a heavy knife to cut all the way through to split the prawn open to butterfly, then remove the black vein.

MUSSELS: At one time, mussels were gritty with sand and needed to be soaked; this is no longer true because mussels are now cultivated on ropes. But they still need to be cleaned. Scrub the mussels clean, pulling off the beards (tufts) and scraping away any barnacles. If any mussels remain open after tapping them on a surface, discard them as they are dead. After cooking, the mussels must be open; if any have remained closed, they should also be discarded.

CRABS: Put the crab in a pan of cold salted water – use about 45g (1½oz) salt to 600ml (1 pint water). Cover and bring to the boil. Reduce the heat and simmer for 15 minutes per 450g (1lb).

Remove the crab and allow to cool. Turn the crab upside down and twist off the legs and claws. Remove the pale belly shell and discard. To clean the crab, remove and discard the small sac at the top of the crab's body and the spongy gills which line the edges. Carefully remove the meat, putting the brown meat and white meat in separate bowls; use a skewer or lobster pick to make removing some of the leg meat easier. Then crack the claws and remove the meat. This is a very fiddly job and can take 15–20 minutes.

SCALLOPS: Carefully prise the shell open with a small strong knife (or oyster knife) and detach the scallop from the lower shell. Scoop out the scallop and discard the frilly white muscle and the dark organs, leaving the orange/pink coral in place. Thoroughly wash the scallop and pat dry with kitchen paper. Scallops need the shortest of cooking times; sear for only 1–2 minutes.

OCTOPUS: Cut the top part of the octopus away from the body and split the top in two; remove the ink sac, entrails, beak and eye. Rinse the tentacles and body under cold water to remove any traces of ink (see page 90 on squid ink). Octopus skin is much tougher to remove than squid skin: first blanch the fish in boiling water for 5 minutes, then cool quickly and scrape off the skin. Pound the octopus a little with a meat mallet to tenderize it before cutting it into small pieces. Octopus is tough fish and therefore needs to be cooked for a long time before it is tender.

SQUID: Remove the tentacles from the main body but do not discard them. Remove and discard the clear-plastic quill that runs through the length of the body and wash the fish clean. Carefully peel away the thin membrane around the outside of the body. Cut away and discard the head and all the innards, but reserve the ink if you need it for the recipe. Wash again, removing any traces of ink. You can cut the body into rings, known as calamari rings. Alternatively, you can cut the body open and place it on a chopping board, inner-side up, and then gently score it in a criss-cross pattern; squid that is prepared this way is for

grilling, barbecuing or stir-fries – it cooks more evenly and curls on cooking. Squid either need to be cooked quickly or for a very long time, otherwise the fish becomes rubbery.

Cooking techniques

You do not need very much specialist equipment for cooking fish and shellfish. A large cooking pan for boiling or a fish kettle are necessary, however. Fish kettles are expensive to buy so if you do not think you're going to use it too often, you can hire one from a fishmonger. Have two or three different-sized ovenproof gratin dishes for poaching or cooking in the oven. Frying pans are crucial – a good heavy-based pan or non-stick variety is essential as is a fish slice to turn the fish over. When deep-frying, you need a frying basket to lower the fish easily into the hot oil; a slotted spoon is also useful for draining deep-fried fish. You should also consider buying a ridged cast-iron grill pan (see page 14) and perhaps a steamer.

Also helpful are tongs, an oyster knife and, of course, a good sharp knife or a filleting knife if you plan to fillet your own fish. If you often barbecue whole fish, fish-shaped or square fish racks to turn the fish would be a practical purchase. If you eat a lot of shellfish, it would be a good idea to purchase a meat mallet for crushing shells and tenderizing tough fish.

BOILING

Although this is one of the easiest methods of cooking fish, you must pay careful attention to the liquid, in this case the Court Bouillon (see page 165). First, it needs to be well seasoned with 10ml (2 teaspoons) of salt. Next, the liquid needs to be brought to just about boiling point before the fish is added. The boiling method is used for cooking lobsters as well as large whole fish such as bass, cod, salmon and turbot.

You may find that using a fish kettle is much easier for boiling and poaching large fish. Bring the Court Bouillon to the boil and boil for 30 minutes. Reduce to a gentle boil, place the fish on a trivet that fits in the fish kettle or wrap in foil or muslin if it is to be served cold. Lower the fish into the boiling liquid and cook for 30 minutes for fish larger than 1kg (2¼lb), or calculate 15 minutes per 500g (1lb 2oz). The fish is perfect when the flesh is opaque and ice white.

POACHING

This type of quick cooking in a little simmering liquid is ideal for all small fish or fillets, especially for types of fish that break up from too much agitation. Prepare a little Court Bouillon following a classic recipe, which includes water, vegetables, herbs, salt and a little white wine (see page 165), or you may poach the fish in Fish Stock (see page 164), wine, water or milk. The fish can either be poached in the oven or on the hob.

For oven cooking, put the fish in a buttered ovenproof dish or roasting tin, add enough court bouillon or other liquid to come halfway up the fish. Cover the dish with foil and cook in the oven for 10–25 minutes, depending on the size of the fish.

For poaching on the hob, place the fish and court bouillon or other liquid in a large shallow frying pan. Bring the liquid to a simmer over a low heat and poach the fish for 5 minutes. Remove from the heat, turn the fish over, cover and leave to stand for 5 minutes for small pieces of fillets or for up to 20 minutes for a whole fish.

Once the fish is removed from the court bouillon or stock, the liquid can be strained through a fine sieve, returned to a clean pan and boiled until reduced to about half, and then used as a base for sauces to be served with the fish.

STEAMING

Very little liquid is required for this cooking technique; this means that the fish steams in its own juices and that way it retains its original flavour and remains tender. Water, Fish Stock (see page 164), a Court Bouillon (see page 165) or white wine are usually used as the steaming liquid. If you like, you can add a sprinkling of lemon juice and some seasoning before steaming. You can use a conventional steamer basket, or you can steam in a rack in a wok or in Chinese steamers. The fish can also be wrapped in greased foil or greaseproof paper beforehand, cooking *en papillote*.

DEEP-FRYING

'Frying is an art,' said Escoffier, 'so it needs a lot of love.' For perfect frying, you need a good deep pan with plenty of surface area to give the fish room to stay separate and not stick to each other as well to achieve a good even colour. You also need a good oil; I like to use olive oil (not extra virgin olive oil) as it gives the fish a good flavour. The oil temperature must be between 180°C/350°F for portioned fish or 200°C/400°F for whole fish. Fish larger than 200g (7oz) need to be filleted before being deep-fried.

There are several ways of preparing fish before deep-frying. One method is to soak the cleaned fish in milk and herbs, drain and pat dry with kitchen paper and then coat in seasoned flour; shake off the excess flour from the fish, then deep-fry until golden. Remove with a slotted spoon and drain on kitchen paper. Another of my favourite methods is to make a smooth batter by mixing together flour and water and seasoning the mixture. Fold whisked egg white into the batter just before using. Coat the fish in the batter, then deep-fry; the fish should be crispy on the outside and soft inside.

To deep-fry crustacea, use the same procedure as for fish. Fry small ones whole, including baby squid. Cut large ones, such as whole squid, into rings.

SHALLOW FRYING

A good frying pan is essential; use one that is heavy-based or non-stick. The type of oil is also important. It needs to be of a good quality; olive oil or extra virgin olive oil are my choice as they add flavour to the fish (sunflower and groundnut are also fine to use). I often add a little butter to help colour and add extra taste.

First, you need to heat the pan and then add the oil. Once the oil is hot, add the butter, if using, and heat until melted and foaming. Add the fish to the pan – don't overcrowd it as you need plenty of space to manoeuvre the fish – and be patient: resist moving the fish around too much. Allow a good colour and crispness to develop on the underside before turning the fish over. For extra crispness, you can flour the fish with seasoned plain flour, making sure to shake off the excess before adding the fish to the pan.

For thick pieces of fillets such as salmon or cod, you can pan-fry the fish on both sides first and then transfer the whole pan to an oven pre-heated to 200°C/400°F/Gas Mark 6 and cook for 5–8 minutes more; this helps cook the fish inside without burning the outside.

STIR-FRYING

This is a fast method of cooking fish. Heat the pan (or wok) before adding and heating the oil until it is very hot. The best fish for stir-frying are those that can be cut into strips and chunks, and also shellfish such as prawns, scallops and squid. Add some vegetables and you have a meal in minutes.

BARBECUING, GRILLING AND CHARGRILLING

Whole fish of all sizes are good for barbecuing, while fish fillets are best to grill as they break up too easily on a barbecue. For both cooking methods, marinate the fish first in an oil-based marinade and then baste it throughout cooking with the marinade. Be sure that the grill or barbecue is very hot before adding the fish. Whole fish need to be scored 2–3 times on both sides to allow good even cooking throughout.

Chargrilling, which is done on a ridged cast-iron grill over charcoal, is also becoming very popular. Fillets of fish, skewers of fish and small whole fish are all perfect for cooking on this pan. It needs to be pre-heated on the hob until almost smoking and the marinated fish added directly on to it, often without brushing the pan first with any extra oil. The food cooks in minutes and has fantastic smoky flavours!

Shellfish such as langoustines, lobsters, prawns, octopus and squid are all good to barbecue, grill or chargrill.

ROASTING MY WAY

This is also a good method for cooking large whole fish or large cuts of fish such as salmon, snapper, loin of swordfish or whole fillet of tuna. Always marinate your fish for a couple of hours with olive oil and herbs before roasting, then use the marinade for cooking the fish in or turn it into a sauce to serve with the fish. When roasting, you can cover the fish with breadcrumbs, salt and black pepper and add some white wine and lemon juice halfway through the cooking time.

The fish needs to roast, uncovered, in an oven pre-heated to about 200°C/400°F/Gas Mark 6 for large fish and 180°C/350°F/Gas Mark 4 for small fish. The hot oven prevents the fish from sticking to the roasting tin as well as giving it a good colour in such a short time of cooking. For cooking times, allow 30–40 minutes for fish weighing about 1kg (2¼lb). Delicate fish such as Dover sole may be covered with buttered foil or greaseproof paper halfway through cooking to keep it from drying out.

Quantities

How much to serve per person is very difficult to calculate, but as a guide allow:

WHOLE FISH: 450g (1lb) per person
FILLETS: 85–115g (3–4oz) fillet per person for a starter and 140–170g (5–6oz) fillet per person for a main course
MOLLUSCS: 450g (1lb) of mussels or clams per person
LARGE CRUSTACEANS: 450g (1lb) of lobster, crab or langoustines per person
SMALL CRUSTACEANS: 340g (12oz) of prawns or shrimps per person

Soups

Zuppa di Cozze

Mussel Soup

Mussels literally cook in minutes – as soon as the shells are open they're done. When making this soup, be sure to keep the cooked mussels covered with cling film to stop them from drying out while you prepare the base for the soup.

Mussels are very inexpensive and therefore perfect for making soup. They also freeze well – scrub them clean and freeze them uncooked in their shells. Before using, thaw them completely, then heat them through.

SERVES 4
PREPARATION TIME: 25 MINUTES
COOKING TIME: 35 MINUTES

1.8kg (4lb) mussels, scrubbed clean, beards and barnacles removed
175ml (6fl oz) dry white wine

85g (3oz) unsalted butter
1 small onion, finely chopped
30g (1oz) plain flour
450ml (15fl oz) Fish Stock (see page 164)
a good pinch of saffron strands
90ml (3fl oz) double cream
salt and freshly ground black pepper

○ Place the mussels in a large heavy-based pan, add half of the wine, cover tightly and cook over a high heat for 3–5 minutes, shaking the pan frequently, until the shells have opened.

○ Strain the pan juices through a fine sieve into a bowl and reserve. Discard any mussels that have remained closed. Reserve 12 of the largest open mussels for the garnish. Remove and discard the shells from the remaining mussels.

○ In a clean pan, melt the butter, add the onion and gently cook for 5 minutes until translucent. Stir in the flour until smooth. Add the remaining wine, reserved pan juices and stock, stirring continuously. Stir in the saffron and gently simmer for about 20 minutes.

○ Pour the soup into a blender or food processor and process until smooth. Return the soup to the pan, add the cream and season to taste. Stir in the shelled mussels and heat them through until the liquid is bubbling.

○ Ladle the soup into 4 warmed bowls and garnish with the reserved mussels. Serve immediately.

Zuppa di Astice Fredda

Chilled Lobster Soup

This soup is loosely based on the famous Spanish soup *Gazpacho* for which hardly any cooking is needed. If you buy your lobster freshly cooked from the fishmonger, then you won't have to do any cooking at all!

Arrange the soup and the lobster mixture in separate bowls and let your guests simply serve themselves.

SERVES 4
PREPARATION TIME: 20 MINUTES PLUS
2 HOURS CHILLING

FOR THE SOUP

675g (1½lb) firm ripe tomatoes, peeled and seeded (see page 26)
½ cucumber, peeled and chopped
3 spring onions, trimmed and chopped
2 fat garlic cloves, crushed
1 red pepper, halved, seeded and chopped
1 green pepper, halved, seeded and chopped
60ml (4 tablespoons) extra virgin olive oil

6 fresh basil leaves
240ml (8fl oz) tomato juice
25ml (1½ tablespoons) red wine vinegar
salt and freshly ground black pepper

TO SERVE

1 x 450g (1lb) cooked lobster
1 small red pepper, halved, seeded and chopped
1 small green pepper, halved, seeded and chopped
½ cucumber, peeled, seeded and finely diced
3 spring onions, trimmed and finely chopped
6 fresh basil leaves

❍ Put all the soup ingredients in a food processor and process until very smooth. Transfer the soup to a large bowl, season to taste, then cover with cling film and chill for at least 2 hours. The soup has to be very well chilled.

❍ Meanwhile, split the lobster down the middle, remove all the meat, including the claw and leg meat, and finely chop. Mix together the lobster, red and green peppers, cucumber and spring onions in a bowl. Tear the basil leaves and add to the lobster mixture. Divide the mixture among 4 serving bowls.

❍ Ladle the soup into 4 chilled bowls and serve separately with the lobster mixture.

Zuppa Orientale

Spiced Prawn Wonton Soup

Because I am based in Soho, near to Chinatown, I have been inspired by the many Chinese supermarkets and restaurants in the area. I tried this oriental-style soup in my fish restaurant and my customers were quite impressed.

You can buy the wonton skins in Chinese supermarkets, oriental hypermarkets and some large supermarkets. However, if they're unavailable or you're short of time, you can use filled ravioli from the supermarket.

Use the Fish Stock on page 164 and add some extra oriental flavourings such as lemon grass and kaffir lime leaves, if you like.

SERVES 4
PREPARATION TIME: 30 MINUTES
COOKING TIME: 10 MINUTES

40 wonton skins
1.2 litres (2 pints) good clear Fish Stock
(see page 164)
salt and freshly ground black pepper

FOR THE FILLING
225g (8oz) raw king prawns, peeled, deveined (see page 11) and finely chopped
125g (4½oz) canned water chestnuts, drained and finely chopped

1 egg, beaten
5ml (1 teaspoon) dry sherry
5ml (1 teaspoon) vegetable oil
15ml (1 tablespoon) cornflour
20 fresh coriander leaves, finely chopped
½ fresh red chilli, seeded and finely chopped

TO SERVE
4 spring onions, trimmed and finely shredded into strips
2.5cm (1in) piece of fresh root ginger, peeled and finely shredded
24 fresh coriander leaves

❍ Put the prawns and chestnuts in a large bowl and mix in the egg, sherry, oil, cornflour, chopped coriander and chilli. Season well to taste.

❍ Place 2.5ml (½ teaspoon) of the prawn mixture in the centre of each wonton, moisten the edges with water, then bring the wonton up and pinch together just above the prawn mixture to form a purse.

❍ Pour the stock into a large pan and bring to a simmer. Fill a separate pan with salted water and bring to the boil. Working in batches, poach the wontons for 2–3 minutes until they float to the surface. Using a slotted spoon, lift out the wontons and place them into the gently simmering stock.

❍ Ladle the soup into 4 warmed bowls and sprinkle with the shredded spring onions and ginger and the coriander leaves.

Crema di Asinello Affumicato e Patate

Cream of Smoked Haddock and Potato Soup

This is a wonderful winter soup. Try adding some parsnips as well – the sweetness of this vegetable will give it a lovely flavour.

Smoked haddock or cod is available dyed or natural. The dyed variety is coloured yellow before smoking, while the natural-coloured smoked fish has no added colour and has a better appearance. Both varieties are widely available at fishmongers and supermarkets.

SERVES 4
PREPARATION TIME: 10 MINUTES
COOKING TIME: 25 MINUTES

85g (3oz) unsalted butter
1 large onion, finely sliced
125g (4½oz) potatoes, peeled and diced

450g (1lb) natural smoked haddock fillet, skinned, pin-boned (see page 10) and diced
1.2 litres (2 pints) milk
90ml (6 tablespoons) chopped fresh flat-leaf parsley
salt and freshly ground white pepper
crusty bread, to serve

❍ Melt the butter in a heavy-based pan, add the onion and cook for 2–3 minutes over a medium heat until soft but not browned. Stir in the potatoes, reduce the heat and cover tightly. Cook for 10 minutes, stirring frequently, until the potatoes are very tender.

❍ Add the haddock to the potato mixture, then stir in the milk and bring to a simmer. Cook for 10–15 minutes until the fish is very tender.

❍ Pour the soup into a blender or food processor and process until completely smooth. Pour the soup back into the pan with half of the parsley and reheat until bubbling, adding seasoning, if required.

❍ Ladle the soup into 4 warmed bowls and sprinkle with the remaining parsley. Serve immediately with crusty bread.

Minestra di Verdura e Granchi

Summer Vegetable and Crab Soup

This is a fabulous flavour combination, and it looks very pretty, too – just right for a casual dinner party in the garden. It needs the minimum of cooking since all these summer vegetables are so tender and juicy when they're in season.

SERVES 4
PREPARATION TIME: 10 MINUTES
COOKING TIME: 20 MINUTES

30g (1oz) butter
1 bay leaf
2 large red-skinned potatoes, peeled and diced
1 medium onion, diced
2 garlic cloves, finely chopped
1 beef tomato, peeled, seeded and diced
(see page 26)

1 courgette, trimmed and diced
225g (8oz) broad beans, shelled
115g (4oz) fresh or frozen peas
30ml (2 tablespoons) chopped fresh flat-leaf parsley
6 fresh mint leaves
6 fresh sage leaves
30ml (2 tablespoons) chopped fresh parsley
1.2 litres (2 pints) Fish Stock (see page 164)
125g (4½oz) fresh white crab meat
salt and freshly ground black pepper
shredded fresh mint leaves, to garnish

○ Melt the butter in a large pan and add the bay leaf, potatoes, onion and garlic. Cover with a piece of damp greaseproof paper (the paper should touch the vegetables) then a tight-fitting lid. Cook (sweat) the vegetables over a low heat for 8–10 minutes until just soft but not browned.

○ Remove the paper. Stir the tomato, courgette, broad beans, peas, and herbs into the potato mixture and cook for 1 minute. Pour in the stock, bring to a simmer and simmer for 5 minutes. Discard the bay leaf and stir in the crab meat. Cook for a further 2–3 minutes until heated through and bubbling. Season to taste.

○ Ladle the soup into 4 warmed bowls and sprinkle with the shredded mint leaves. Serve immediately.

Minestra di Ceci e Pancetta con Triglie

Chick Pea and Pancetta Broth with Red Mullet

Red mullet is probably my favourite fish. Most people are put off by its fine bones, but if you get your fishmonger to fillet it for you, it should have no bones at all. As an extra precaution, run your fingers along the flesh of the fillet: if you feel a bone, pull it out with a pair of tweezers – this is known as 'pin-boning' (see page 10).
Red mullet is perfect for this recipe as it has a good strong flavour and combines well with the pancetta. If pancetta is unavailable, use smoked bacon instead.

SERVES 4
PREPARATION TIME: 20 MINUTES
COOKING TIME: 35 MINUTES

30ml (2 tablespoons) olive oil
125g (4½oz) pancetta, cut into matchsticks
1 bay leaf, torn in half
5ml (1 teaspoon) chopped fresh rosemary leaves
a pinch of saffron strands
1 small dried red chilli, crumbled
1 garlic clove, finely chopped
1 medium onion, finely chopped
1 stick celery, trimmed and finely chopped
1 carrot, finely diced

2 litres (3½ pints) Fish Stock (see page 164)
2 x 400g (14oz) cans chick peas, drained and rinsed
1 large potato, peeled and roughly grated
4 x 225g (8oz) red mullet, filleted and pin-boned (see page 10)
15ml (1 tablespoon) vegetable oil
salt and freshly ground black pepper

TO GARNISH AND SERVE
extra virgin olive oil
roughly chopped fresh flat-leaf parsley
lemon wedges

❍ Heat the olive oil in a large pan, add the pancetta and cook over a low heat for 4–5 minutes until just beginning to turn golden brown. Stir in the bay leaf, rosemary, saffron, chilli, garlic, onion, celery and carrot. Cook for 5 minutes until all the vegetables are soft.

❍ Pour the stock into the pan and add the chick peas and grated potato. Bring to a simmer and cook for 15–20 minutes until the potato has disintegrated and the soup is thickened. Season to taste.

❍ Heat a heavy-based frying pan until very hot. Season the fish, lightly brush with the vegetable oil and cook for 2–3 minutes on each side – the fish should be just tender and beginning to turn golden brown.

❍ Ladle the soup into 4 large, shallow, warmed bowls and top each with two fillets. Drizzle with the extra virgin olive oil and sprinkle with the flat-leaf parsley. Serve with lemon wedges.

Zuppa alla Marinara

Fisherman's Soup

This type of fish soup is popular in coastal regions and there are numerous versions, but no hard and fast rules. Just make sure that the fish is as fresh as possible and use a good variety. As an alternative to the fish used here, you could include a selection of fillets such as red mullet, monkfish, cod or bream.

Around the Adriatic sea, fish soup is called *brodetto*; it's traditionally served with bread baked in oil, called *casada*, but any good peasant bread will do.

The soup makes a delicious starter, but because it is filling you could also serve it for a light supper.

SERVES 4
PREPARATION TIME: 30 MINUTES PLUS
30 MINUTES SOAKING
COOKING TIME: 45 MINUTES

500g (1lb 2oz) clams or mussels
60ml (4 tablespoons) olive oil
2 garlic cloves, finely chopped
1 shallot, finely chopped
450g (1lb) squid, cleaned (see page 12) and cut into rings
900ml (1½ pints) Fish Stock (see page 164)
150ml (5fl oz) white wine

1 x 400g (14oz) can borlotti beans, drained and rinsed
225g (8oz) medium-sized raw prawns, peeled and deveined (see page 11)
sprig of fresh rosemary
15g (½oz) fresh coriander
15g (½oz) fresh flat-leaf parsley
15ml (1 tablespoon) cornflour
30ml (2 tablespoons) cold water
5ml (1 teaspoon) salt
5ml (1 teaspoon) freshly ground black pepper
juice of 1 lime
peasant bread, to serve

❍ If using clams, soak them in salted water for 30 minutes to remove the grit, then wash in clean water and drain. If using mussels, scrub them clean and remove the beards and barnacles.

❍ Heat half of the oil in a heavy-based deep pan and sauté the garlic and shallot for 3 minutes until just golden. Add the squid and cook over a medium heat for 3 minutes. Add the stock and simmer for 20 minutes.

❍ Meanwhile, put the clams or mussels and the wine in a separate large heavy-based pan. Cover tightly and cook over a high heat for 3–5 minutes, shaking the pan frequently, until all the shells have opened.

❍ Strain the pan juices through a fine sieve, then add to the squid. Add the beans to the squid and simmer for 5–8 minutes.

○ Meanwhile, remove the shells from the mussels or clams, discarding any that have remained closed. Stir the mussels or clams, prawns, the rosemary, coriander and parsley and the remaining oil into the squid mixture. Simmer for a further 10 minutes.

○ Mix together the cornflour and water to form a paste and add it to the squid mixture. Stir over a gentle heat for 2 minutes until the soup is just thickened and no longer cloudy. Season to taste with salt and black pepper and the lime juice.

○ Ladle the soup into 4 warmed bowls and serve immediately with peasant bread.

Zuppa di Cozze e Sarde

Sardine and Mussel Soup

This soup is quite unusual. In Italy we call it 'poor man's soup' as these ingredients are inexpensive and very easy to find – why not try it out on your family!
Another traditional way of serving fish soups in Italy, especially the more rustic type, is to put a thick slice of toast in the bottom of the soup bowl before adding the soup or broth – it makes it more satisfying at the end, especially with all those brilliant flavours.

SERVES 4
PREPARATION TIME: 25 MINUTES
COOKING TIME: 30 MINUTES

2kg (4½lb) mussels, scrubbed clean, beards and barnacles removed
45–60ml (3–4 tablespoons) water
4 x 125g (4½oz) sardines, filleted
75ml (5 tablespoons) extra virgin olive oil

1 small onion, finely chopped
120ml (4fl oz) dry white wine
30ml (2 tablespoons) finely chopped fresh flat-leaf parsley
5ml (1 teaspoon) tomato purée
1 strip of lemon zest
4 slices thick crusty bread
1 garlic clove, halved
salt and freshly ground black pepper

○ Put the mussels and water in a large heavy-based pan. Cover tightly and cook over a high heat for 3–5 minutes, shaking the pan frequently, until the shells have opened.

○ Strain the pan juices through a fine sieve into a bowl and reserve. Discard any mussels that have remained closed. Reserve one-third of the mussels in their shells. Remove and discard the shells from the remaining mussels, then chop the shelled mussels and set aside.

○ Place the sardines in a large frying pan and cover with cold water. Gently bring to the boil and cook for 5 minutes until tender. Drain and reserve the pan juices. Chop or finely flake the sardines.

○ Heat 60ml (4 tablespoons) of the oil in a deep pan and sauté the onion for 3 minutes until lightly browned. Add the chopped mussels and sardines and the wine and parsley. Blend in the tomato purée, lemon zest, reserved mussel and sardine pan juices, and enough boiling water to obtain 1 litre (1¾ pints) of broth. Season to taste and simmer for about 10 minutes.

○ Meanwhile, pre-heat the grill to medium. Rub the bread slices with the halved garlic and brush with the remaining oil. Place the slices on the grill pan and toast until golden brown on both sides.

○ Add the reserved mussels to the soup and cook for a further 5 minutes. Remove and discard the lemon zest and adjust the seasoning. Put a slice of toast in each of 4 warmed bowls and ladle the broth and fish over the top. Serve immediately.

Stufato di Vongole e Granturco

Clam and Corn Chowder

Sweetcorn and clams have been a favourite combination of mine for a long time, but feel free to use other vegetables such as courgettes – whatever is in season. Clams are available all year round. Opt for the smaller variety of clams for this soup, such as *palourde* (Venus) or the Littlenecks or cherrystone.

SERVES 4
PREPARATION TIME: 30 MINUTES PLUS
30 MINUTES SOAKING
COOKING TIME: 30 MINUTES

24 small clams
30g (1oz) butter
1 large onion, finely chopped
1 garlic clove, finely chopped
2 sticks celery, trimmed and finely chopped
1 medium carrot, diced
225g (8oz) potato, peeled and diced

2 sprigs of fresh thyme
1 bay leaf
55g (2oz) pancetta, diced
2 sweetcorns on the cob, leaves and tassels removed
600ml (1 pint) milk
300ml (10fl oz) double cream
30ml (2 tablespoons) dry white wine
30ml (2 tablespoons) chopped fresh parsley
1 red pepper, roasted, peeled, seeded and diced (see page 171)

❍ Soak the clams in salted water for 30 minutes to remove the grit, then wash in clean water and drain.

❍ Melt the butter in a large deep pan and add the onion, garlic, celery, carrot, potato, thyme, bay leaf and pancetta. Cover with a damp piece of greaseproof paper (the paper should touch the vegetables) then a tight-fitting lid. Cook (sweat) the vegetables over a low heat for 5–7 minutes, shaking the pan occasionally, until just tender but not browned. Remove the paper.

❍ Meanwhile, stand a sweetcorn cob on a chopping board and cut down the sides to release the kernels. Repeat with the second sweetcorn cob. Add the kernels and milk to the vegetable mixture and simmer for 8–10 minutes. Remove and discard the thyme and bay leaf.

❍ Pour half of the soup into a food processor and process until smooth. Return to the rest of the soup in the pan and add the cream and wine. Simmer for 5–8 minutes.

❍ Meanwhile, place the clams in a steamer or in a colander set over a pan of simmering water. Cover tightly and steam for 5 minutes to open. Discard any clams that have remained closed. Remove and discard the shells.

❍ Stir the clams, parsley and red pepper into the soup. Heat through until bubbling. Season to taste.

❍ Ladle the soup into 4 warmed bowls and serve immediately.

Pasta e Fagioli al Baccalà

Pasta, Cannellini Beans and Salt Cod Soup

This soup is based on the traditional *Pasta Fagioli*, to which I have added fish. Salt cod is simply cod that has been salted and dried for preservation. Once salt cod is soaked in many changes of cold water (to reconstitute it and remove the excess salt) and cooked, it again resembles fresh cod with large tender flakes. However, the flavour is richer than ordinary cod, and this makes it perfect for soups or for other dishes where a strong sauce is going to be used. In this case, the mellow flavour of the roasted garlic is absolutely ideal.

Salt cod is now widely available in supermarkets – find it close to either the West Indian ingredients or tinned fish. If you opt not to use salt cod, you can make this soup with fresh cod, but cook it for about 10 minutes once it has been added to the soup.

Dried pasta for soup, often referred to as pasta for minestrone, comes in tiny shapes, which include stars, ridged or smooth quills and baby macaroni (*maccheroncini*). They are added directly to the broth and cooked with all the other ingredients, acting a little like a thickener.

SERVES 4
PREPARATION TIME: 30 MINUTES
COOKING TIME: 1 HOUR 10 MINUTES

1 garlic bulb
30ml (2 tablespoons) extra virgin olive oil
1 beef tomato
1 medium onion, diced
1 carrot, diced
1 leek, cut into 4 lengthways and diced

1 bay leaf
2 x 415g (14½oz) cans cannellini beans, drained and rinsed
1.4 litres (2½ pints) Fish Stock (see page 164)
450g (1lb) salt cod, soaked overnight in plenty of cold water, then drained
125g (4½oz) dried pasta for soup
30ml (2 tablespoons) chopped fresh flat-leaf parsley
freshly ground black pepper

○ Pre-heat the oven to 200°C/400°F/Gas Mark 6.

○ Brush the garlic bulb with a little of the oil then wrap loosely in foil. Roast in the oven for 30–40 minutes until the bulb is very tender. Unwrap the garlic and cut it in half, squeeze out the pulp into a sieve, then push it through to purée.

○ Meanwhile, core the tomato and score an x at the bottom. Blanch in boiling water for about 15 seconds, then drain and place in iced water for about 5 seconds. Remove the tomato from the water and, using a small sharp knife, peel off the skin. Cut the tomato in half horizontally and squeeze out the seeds. Place the tomato halves, cut-side down, on a chopping board and cut into strips, then cut across the strips to dice the flesh.

○ Heat the remaining oil in a deep pan and add the onion, carrot, leek and bay leaf. Gently cook for 4–5 minutes to soften the vegetables. Add the beans, stock and tomato and cook the soup for a further 15 minutes.

○ Meanwhile, cut the salt cod into 1cm (½in) cubes. Remove and discard the bay leaf from the soup mixture. Pour one-third of the soup into a food processor, process until smooth, then return to the remaining soup in the pan. Stir in the garlic purée and the salt cod.

○ Simmer the soup for 20 minutes, then add the pasta and cook for a further 10 minutes until the salt cod is very tender and flakes easily and the pasta is al dente.

○ Stir the parsley into the soup and season with plenty of black pepper – it's unlikely that you'll need any extra salt as the cod will have quite a strong and slightly salty flavour.

○ Ladle the soup into 4 warmed bowls and serve immediately.

Zuppa di Salmone e Spinaci

Salmon and Spinach Soup

This recipe was invented in one of my restaurants by mistake. A small party had ordered grilled salmon with spinach and then changed their minds, so we made a soup out of it for the staff and everybody loved it. The ingredients are based on a classic combination of ingredients.

SERVES 4
PREPARATION TIME: 15 MINUTES
COOKING TIME: 20 MINUTES

30g (1oz) butter
1 garlic clove, finely chopped
1 red onion, finely diced
1 stick celery, trimmed and finely diced
1 fennel bulb, cut into 4 lengthways, hard core removed, ends trimmed and
cut into small rounds.

450g (1lb) waxy new potatoes, peeled and quartered lengthways
1.4 litres (2½ pints) Fish Stock (see page 164)
225g (8oz) salmon fillet, skinned and cut into 1cm (½in) cubes
275ml (9fl oz) crème fraîche
125g (4½oz) baby spinach, washed and drained
salt and freshly ground black pepper
fresh lemon juice, to taste

❍ Melt the butter in a heavy-based deep pan, add the garlic, onion, celery and fennel and cook for 2–3 minutes until soft but not browned.

❍ Add the potatoes and cook for 1 minute. Pour in the stock, bring to a simmer and simmer for 10 minutes until the potatoes are tender. Add the salmon and simmer for 1–2 minutes.

❍ Stir in the crème fraîche and then the spinach. Season well with salt and black pepper and a little lemon juice. Heat through for 1–2 minutes – the spinach should just be wilted.

❍ Ladle the soup into 4 warmed bowls and serve immediately.

Zuppa di Pomodori Arrosti e Capesante

Roast Tomato and Scallop Soup

Whether you are grilling, stir-frying or poaching scallops, you should always keep the cooking time to a minimum or else the succulent flesh will become tough. If you use frozen scallops for this recipe, do not thaw them before adding them to the pan. Choose tomatoes that have a good flavour for this soup; I find that the tomatoes sold on the vine are some of the best-tasting ones available. Very ripe plum tomatoes are also good. However, organic ripe tomatoes would be perfect!

SERVES 4
PREPARATION TIME: 20 MINUTES
COOKING TIME: 30 MINUTES

1.8kg (4lb) ripe tomatoes, quartered
1 medium onion, sliced
2 garlic cloves, finely chopped

120ml (8 tablespoons) extra virgin olive oil
15ml (1 tablespoon) balsamic vinegar
20 fresh basil leaves
225g (8oz) queen scallops, trimmed with roes removed, washed and patted dry
sea salt flakes and freshly ground black pepper
roughly torn fresh basil leaves, to garnish (optional)

❍ Pre-heat the oven to 200°C/400°F/Gas Mark 6.

❍ Put the tomatoes, onion and garlic in a large roasting tin. Sprinkle with sea salt flakes, black pepper, half of the oil and all the vinegar. Roast for 20–30 minutes until soft and just beginning to caramelize in places.

❍ Transfer the tomato mixture to a food processor with another 45ml (3 tablespoons) of the oil and the basil leaves and process to a purée. Strain the soup through a sieve, discarding the skin and seeds of the tomatoes. Pour the soup into a deep pan and heat through gently until bubbling, adjusting the seasoning, if necessary.

❍ Meanwhile, heat the remaining oil in a large frying pan and add the scallops. Stir-fry for 1–2 minutes, until just tinged golden on the outside. Season to taste

❍ Ladle the soup into 4 warmed bowls and spoon the scallops over the top. Serve immediately, garnished with the basil leaves, if desired.

Starters

Frittura di Gamberi e Melanzane

Fried Prawns and Aubergines

I love the combination of fried fish and vegetables. You can substitute any vegetables of your choice for the aubergines – peppers and courgettes would make excellent alternatives.

SERVES 4
PREPARATION TIME: 15 MINUTES PLUS
15 MINUTES STANDING
COOKING TIME: 10 MINUTES

1 large aubergine
15ml (1 tablespoon) salt
4 eggs
5ml (1 teaspoon) freshly ground black pepper
15ml (1 tablespoon) chopped fresh oregano
30ml (2 tablespoons) plain flour

30ml (2 tablespoons) extra virgin olive oil
3 garlic cloves, finely chopped
12 raw Mediterranean prawns, peeled and deveined (see page 11)
120ml (8 tablespoons) Lemon Mayonnaise (see page 166)
55g (2oz) capers
15ml (1 tablespoon) chopped fresh flat-leaf parsley
vegetable oil for deep-frying
lemon wedges, to serve

❍ Trim the ends from the aubergine and cut it crossways into 12 thin slices. Place the slices in a colander and sprinkle with the salt. Set the colander on a plate to catch the juices, then leave to stand for 15 minutes. Rinse the slices under cold water and pat dry with kitchen paper.

❍ Put the eggs, a little black pepper and the oregano in a bowl and lightly beat with a fork. Spread the flour on a flat plate and season with the rest of the black pepper.

❍ Pour enough vegetable oil for deep-frying into a deep frying pan over a medium heat. Heat until a piece of bread dropped in the oil sizzles and turns golden brown in 30 seconds.

❍ Working in batches, coat the aubergine slices in the seasoned flour and then in the egg mixture and deep-fry for 2–3 minutes until golden on both sides. Using a slotted spoon, transfer the slices to kitchen paper to drain.

❍ Meanwhile, heat the olive oil in a shallow frying pan and fry the garlic for 1 minute. Add the prawns and cook for 2 minutes on each side.

❍ Place 3 aubergine slices on 4 serving plates and top each with a prawn. Spoon over the oil and garlic juices from the prawns. Mix together the lemon mayonnaise and the capers and season to taste. Place a dollop on each plate and sprinkle with parsley. Serve with lemon wedges.

Avocado al Granchio Gratin

Avocado Stuffed with Crab Gratin

Avocados are normally served cold, but if you find them becoming over-ripe this is a great way of using them. This method of removing the stone is foolproof. This dish can be prepared and cooked in no time at all, but it will make a wonderful impression.

SERVES 4
PREPARATION TIME: 5 MINUTES
COOKING TIME: 2 MINUTES

2 large ripe avocados
125g (4½oz) fresh crab meat
1 medium egg yolk
30ml (2 tablespoons) chopped fresh basil leaves

30ml (2 tablespoons) chopped fresh coriander leaves
10ml (2 teaspoons) single cream
juice of ½ lemon
30ml (2 tablespoons) freshly grated Parmesan cheese
salt and freshly ground black pepper
radicchio leaves to garnish

❍ Using a sharp thin-bladed knife, cut each avocado in half, cutting around the stone. Twist each half in opposite directions and pull the halves away to separate. Pierce the stone with the side of the knife blade, then twist and lift out the stone. Scoop the flesh into a bowl, being careful not to tear the skin, and reserve the shells.

❍ Put the crab meat into the bowl with the avocado and beat in the egg yolk, herbs, cream and lemon juice. Season to taste.

❍ Pre-heat the grill to hot.

❍ Spoon the mixture back into the avocado shells and sprinkle with Parmesan cheese. Place the avocados on the grill pan and grill for 2 minutes until the cheese begins to melt.

❍ Place the avocado halves on warmed serving plates and garnish with the radicchio leaves. Serve immediately, sprinkled with extra black pepper.

Calamari alla Brace

Chargrilled Squid with Red Pepper Salsa

This dish is very popular in all my restaurants, where it's either served as a starter or a light main course for lunch.

The squid is scored to tenderize it and also to make it curl during cooking. Squid comes in different sizes: if they are small then leave them whole, otherwise slice them after cooking so that they look more appetizing. The squid needs the minimum of cooking in this recipe – don't overcook it or it will turn rubbery.

SERVES 4
PREPARATION TIME: 30 MINUTES
COOKING TIME: 6–8 MINUTES

8 medium-sized squid, cleaned (see page 12)
90ml (6 tablespoons) extra virgin olive oil
sea salt flakes and freshly ground black pepper
lemon wedges, to serve

FOR THE RED PEPPER SALSA
1 red pepper, peeled, seeded and finely diced (see page 171)

1 small fresh red chilli, roasted, peeled, seeded and chopped
grated zest and juice of 1 lime
15ml (1 tablespoon) chopped fresh coriander leaves
15ml (1 tablespoon) chopped fresh flat-leaf parsley
salt and freshly ground black pepper

FOR THE SALAD
250g (9oz) wild rocket, washed and drained
drizzling of extra virgin olive oil
drizzling of balsamic vinegar

○ Separate the tentacles from the main body of the squid. Cut open the main body cavity. Using a thin-bladed knife, score the inside of the squid with diagonal lines at regular 1cm (½in) intervals. Turn the squid at a 90 degree angle and repeat the scoring to give diamond cuts.

○ Pre-heat the grill to medium-hot.

○ Place the squid, scored-side down, on a foil-lined grill pan, brush with a little of the oil, then sprinkle with sea salt. Add the squid tentacles and grill for 3–4 minutes. Turn the squid over, brush with a little more oil and sprinkle with sea salt. Grill for a further 3–4 minutes until the squid curls up and is tender. Halve each piece of scored squid.

○ Meanwhile, mix together the red pepper, chilli, lime zest and juice, salt and black pepper, coriander, parsley and remaining oil.

○ Put the rocket in a bowl, toss with oil and vinegar and season to taste. Place the rocket on a platter or 4 serving plates and arrange the squid (left whole or sliced) around the rocket. Spoon the salsa over the squid and serve immediately with lemon wedges.

Cozze Ripiene

Stuffed Mussels

As you've noticed, there are many recipes with mussels in this book, but they're such wonderful shellfish and so easy to find!
For a more sophisticated presentation, use the large New Zealand green-lipped mussels; they're much larger in size and you'll only need two mussels per serving. Arrange them on plates with a small salad of green and red chicory drizzled with a lemon and honey dressing.

SERVES 4
PREPARATION TIME: 30 MINUTES
COOKING TIME: 10 MINUTES

30ml (2 tablespoons) extra virgin olive oil
4 spring onions, trimmed and finely chopped
4 garlic cloves, finely chopped
450g (1lb) large mussels, scrubbed clean, beards and barnacles removed

150ml (5fl oz) dry white wine
4 thick rashers smoked bacon
225g (8oz) baby spinach, washed and drained
30ml (2 tablespoons) dried breadcrumbs
15g (½oz) fresh flat-leaf parsley, finely chopped
2 large sprigs of fresh rosemary, stalks discarded and leaves finely chopped
1 medium egg, beaten
salt and freshly ground black pepper

❍ Heat half of the oil in a deep heavy-based pan, add half of the spring onions and half of the garlic and sauté for 1 minute.

❍ Add the mussels and wine, cover tightly and cook over a high heat, shaking the pan frequently, for 3–5 minutes until the shells have opened. Discard any mussels that have remained the closed.

❍ Remove and discard half of the shell of each mussel. Place the mussels in their half shell on a baking tray and cover with cling film to prevent them from drying out.

❍ Meanwhile, pre-heat the grill to medium. Place the bacon on the grill pan and grill, turning, until crisp, then finely dice.

❍ Place the spinach in a colander and stand it in the sink. Pour a kettle full of hot water over it – it will just wilt. When cold enough to handle, roughly chop the spinach and mix in a bowl with the remaining spring onions and garlic. Add the bacon, half of the breadcrumbs and half of the herbs. Season to taste. Stir in the egg to bind.

❍ Take each mussel out of its shell and fill the shell with the stuffing. Replace the mussel and sprinkle with the remaining breadcrumbs and herbs. Drizzle with the remaining oil. Place the mussels on the grill pan and grill under a hot grill for 2–3 minutes until the breadcrumbs are golden brown. Serve immediately.

Frittura di Bianchetti e Fiori di Zucchina

Deep-Fried Whitebait with Courgette Flowers

Whitebait is the general name given to tiny fish that often include herring and sprat. They are perfect floured and deep-fried until crisp and eaten whole. Here I've seasoned them with paprika. I like to use smoked paprika which is available at good Italian and Spanish delis.

Courgette flowers are sold still attached to baby courgettes. These are quite expensive and only good when in season, therefore reserve them for special occasions. Use sliced courgettes or halved baby courgettes when the flowers are not available.

SERVES 4
PREPARATION TIME: 25 MINUTES PLUS
5 MINUTES SOAKING
COOKING TIME: 15 MINUTES

8 courgettes with their flowers
600ml (1 pint) milk
15ml (1 tablespoon) salt

450g (1lb) whitebait, cleaned and patted dry
55g (2oz) plain flour
15ml (1 tablespoon) paprika
salt and freshly ground black pepper
vegetable oil for deep-frying
sea salt flakes, to sprinkle
1 quantity Garlic Mayonnaise (see page 166),
to serve

❍ Leaving the flower attached, cut the courgettes in half. Pour the milk into a large bowl and add 15ml (1 tablespoon) of salt. Add the courgettes and flowers for 30 seconds, then, using a slotted spoon, remove the courgettes and flowers and pat dry with kitchen paper.

❍ Add the whitebait to the salted milk and soak for 5 minutes. Drain and discard the milk. Pat the whitebait dry with kitchen paper. Spread the flour on a flat plate and season with paprika and salt and black pepper.

❍ Pour enough vegetable oil for deep-frying into a deep frying pan over a medium heat. Heat until a piece of bread dropped in the oil sizzles and turns brown in 30 seconds.

❍ Working in batches, coat the fish in the seasoned flour and deep-fry for 2–3 minutes until crisp and golden. Using a slotted spoon, transfer the fish to kitchen paper to soak up the excess oil. Repeat with the courgette flowers, ensuring that they're closed before adding them to the oil. Deep-fry for 1 minute until crisp and golden. Drain on kitchen paper.

❍ Divide the whitebait and courgettes among serving plates and sprinkle with the sea salt. Serve immediately with garlic mayonnaise.

Gamberoni alla Diavola

Devilled Prawns

As their name – *diavola* – says, these prawns are a little spicy. Serve them very simply: just arrange them on a plate and spoon over their juices – they make perfect finger food. Accompany with crusty bread to mop up all the juices.

You can use any type of large prawn – tiger or Mediterranean. Be sure that the prawns are raw, otherwise they may toughen too much when they're cooked.

SERVES 4
COOKING TIME: 30 MINUTES
PREPARATION TIME: 15 MINUTES

12 raw jumbo prawns
60ml (4 tablespoons) sunflower oil
55g (2oz) unsalted butter

6 garlic cloves, finely chopped
2 fresh red chillies, seeded and sliced into rings
1 bunch spring onions, trimmed and finely chopped
200ml (7fl oz) dry white wine
5ml (1 teaspoon) salt
5ml (1 teaspoon) freshly ground black pepper

❍ Remove the heads from the prawns, then peel the shells, leaving the tail end intact. Using a sharp knife, gently cut around the outside curve of the prawn and remove the black vein. To butterfly the prawns, cut all the way through, stopping at the tail but keeping the shells still intact.

❍ Heat the sunflower oil in a large pan, then add the prawns, which should be opened out with the tails sticking up. Cook for 2 minutes, shaking the pan occasionally, and then cook for another 2 minutes until the prawns are bright pink. Transfer the prawns to a plate and set aside.

❍ Drain the oil from the pan, then add the butter and heat until frothy. Stir in the garlic, chillies and spring onions and cook for 2 minutes over a high heat. Stir in the wine and bring to the boil.

❍ Return the prawns to the pan, season with the salt and pepper and simmer for 4 minutes over a low heat. Serve immediately.

Polipo alla Casalinga

Octopus with Fresh Tomatoes, Chilli and White Wine

It seems that many people are scared of cooking octopus. But you can leave the cleaning to the fishmonger and all you'll have to do is cut it to the size or shape required (however see page 12 where I explain how to prepare it yourself). Octopus needs to be cooked for quite a while to tenderize it – hence the name of the recipe 'home-made octopus', as housewives had the time to stew this cephalopod for ages! Italian seafood starters vary enormously, and so depending on the time of year, you don't have to follow this recipe to the letter. You can easily substitute squid for octopus – simply poach the squid for a few minutes, drain, then continue as below. Accompany this dish with a small rocket and Parmesan cheese salad.

SERVES 4
PREPARATION TIME: 20 MINUTES
COOKING TIME: 1 HOUR

1.35kg (3lb) octopus, cleaned (see page 12)
1 medium onion, halved
2 celery sticks, trimmed and chopped
4 bay leaves
15g (½oz) fresh dill
30ml (2 tablespoons) extra virgin olive oil
4 spring onions, trimmed and finely chopped
2 garlic cloves, crushed

1 fresh red chilli, seeded and finely chopped
450g (1lb) plum tomatoes, peeled and chopped
(see page 26)
150ml (5fl oz) dry white wine
150ml (5fl oz) Fish Stock (see page 164)
55g (2oz) pitted black olives
salt and freshly ground black pepper

TO SERVE
extra virgin olive oil
lime wedges

❍ Cut the main body of the octopus into rings and the tentacles into 5cm (2in) lengths. Put the octopus, onion, celery, bay leaves and 2 sprigs of the dill in a pan of cold water. Bring to the boil, skimming the surface of any scum. Reduce to a simmer and cook for 45 minutes until the octopus is tender. Do not boil the octopus rapidly as this can make it tough. Drain, discarding the cooking liquid and flavourings.

❍ Heat the oil in a separate pan. When hot, add the spring onions, garlic and chilli and sauté for

1 minute. Add the tomatoes and simmer for a further 5 minutes. Add the wine and stock and simmer for 5 minutes more.

❍ Finely chop the remaining dill and add to the spring onion mixture, then add the cooked octopus and black olives. Season to taste.

❍ Serve the octopus warm or cold, drizzled with oil and accompanied by lime wedges.

Sformatini di Granchi e Zucchine

Crab and Courgette Tart

This wonderful tart needs to come out of the oven when the filling is just set as it will simply carry on cooking – the end result will be a moist creamy filling with a crisp pastry. Ideally prepare it just before it's required.

For a starter, cut the tart into thin wedges and serve with a salad garnish. For a lunch, cut the tart into 4 and serve with a more substantial mixed leaf salad and chopped fresh tomatoes dressed with extra virgin olive oil and basil leaves.

Use baby courgettes with flowers for a special occasion; at other times use normal courgettes (1 medium courgette will be plenty).

SERVES 4–6
PREPARATION TIME: 30 MINUTES PLUS
30 MINUTES CHILLING AND
15 MINUTES RESTING
COOKING TIME: 40 MINUTES

200g (7oz) plain flour
a good pinch of salt
125g (4½oz) unsalted butter, diced and chilled
2 medium egg yolks
15–30ml (1–2 tablespoons) ice-cold water

FOR THE FILLING
200ml (7fl oz) milk
4 medium eggs, lightly beaten
200ml (7fl oz) double cream
2 pinches of freshly grated nutmeg
4 courgettes with their flowers
170g (6oz) fresh white crab meat
125g (4½oz) gruyère cheese, grated
salt and freshly ground black pepper

❍ Put the flour, salt and butter in a food processor and pulse until the mixture resembles coarse bread-crumbs. Add the egg yolks and water and process until a dough is formed. Remove the dough, wrap in cling film and chill for 30 minutes.

❍ Pre-heat the oven to 200°C/400°F/Gas Mark 6.

❍ Roll out the pastry on a lightly floured surface and use to line a 23cm (9in) round fluted, loose-based tart tin. Prick the base with a fork, line the base and sides with greaseproof paper and fill with baking beans. Bake the pastry case blind for 15 minutes. Remove the lining and beans.

❍ Meanwhile, mix together the milk, eggs, cream and nutmeg in a bowl. Season to taste.

❍ Remove the flowers from the courgettes and set aside. Coarsely grate the courgettes and add them to the cream mixture. Stir in the crab. Spoon the filling into the pastry case.

❍ Split the courgette flowers in half lengthways and arrange around the rim of the tart. Sprinkle over the cheese and bake for about 25 minutes until the filling is just set and the surface is golden brown. Allow to rest for 15 minutes before serving.

Capesante all'Orientale

Queen Scallops in Crispy Pastry

I invented this wonderful dish when I was shopping in Chinatown. I was buying vegetables for my restaurant and I made it up on the spot. In my restaurant I use spring roll pastry, which is available in the freezer section of large supermarkets and in Chinese supermarkets. However, I've adapted this recipe for you to use filo pastry, which is available everywhere fresh or frozen.

SERVES 4
PREPARATION TIME: 20 MINUTES
COOKING TIME: 5 MINUTES

3 sheets filo pastry
12 queen scallops, trimmed with roes removed
5ml (1 teaspoon) five-spice powder
12 large fresh coriander leaves
30ml (2 tablespoons) plain flour
45–60ml (3–4 tablespoons) cold water
salt and freshly ground black pepper
vegetable oil for deep-frying

FOR THE DIPPING SAUCE
120ml (4fl oz) soy sauce
1 small fresh red chilli, sliced into rings
juice of ½ lemon
1 small garlic clove, crushed

TO SERVE
grated mooli
pickled ginger
shredded spring onions

❍ Cut the sheets of filo pastry into 12cm x 10cm (5in x 4in) squares. Cover with cling film or a damp tea towel to prevent the pastry from drying out.

❍ Season the scallops with the five-spice powder and salt and black pepper. Take one square of pastry and put a coriander leaf in the centre, then top with a scallop. Mix together the flour and water to form a paste. Brush the pastry edges with the paste, then bring the pastry up and pinch together just above the scallop to form a purse.

❍ Pour enough oil for deep-frying into a deep frying pan over a medium heat. Heat until a piece of bread dropped in the oil sizzles and turns golden brown in 30 seconds.

❍ Working in batches, add the scallop filo purses to the oil and deep-fry for 1–2 minutes until golden brown and crisp. Using a slotted spoon, transfer the purses to kitchen paper to drain.

❍ Mix together the soy sauce, chilli, lemon juice and garlic, then divide among 4 small dipping bowls. Serve the scallop purses warm with the sauce, accompanied by the grated mooli, pickled ginger and shredded spring onions.

Pâté di Pesce Tricolore

Smoked Mackerel and Salmon Pâté

Alonzo, one of my chefs, prepared this for a christening party and it was the first dish that disappeared from the buffet. Although the instructions might seem a little complicated, the pâté is surprisingly simple to make, and also lots of fun. The pears, which were used by the Moors, who influenced Sicilian cooking, add a luscious texture and flavour to the dish.

SERVES 4
PREPARATION TIME: 45 MINUTES PLUS
1 HOUR CHILLING
COOKING TIME: 15 MINUTES

3 pears, peeled, cored and sliced
450g (1lb) salmon fillets
2 sprigs of fresh parsley
1 bay leaf
1 celery stick, trimmed and roughly chopped
6 large spinach leaves, tough stalks removed,
then washed

340g (12oz) peppered mackerel fillets,
skin removed
2 garlic cloves, crushed
300ml (10fl oz) double cream
15g (½oz) fresh basil
450ml (15fl oz) Fish Stock (see page 164)
30ml (2 tablespoons) aspic
salt and freshly ground black pepper

TO SERVE
endive leaves
Red Pepper Salsa (see page 171)

❍ Bring a medium pan of water to a simmer and add the pear slices. Scrunch up a piece of greaseproof paper and place it on top of the pears, then cover tightly and simmer for 10 minutes until tender. Remove from the heat and let stand, covered, for 10 minutes. Remove the greaseproof paper and, using a slotted spoon, transfer the pear slices to a plate to cool.

❍ Meanwhile, place the salmon fillets, skin-side down, in a large frying pan and cover with cold water. Add the parsley sprigs, bay leaf and celery. Gently bring to the boil, remove from the heat, cover and let stand for 10 minutes. The salmon should be tender and just flaking but still just pink in the centre. Remove the salmon from the poaching liquid and allow to cool.

❍ Bring a small pan of water to the boil. Add the spinach and cook for 1 minute, taking care not to break the leaves. Drain and cool under cold water, then pat dry with kitchen paper.

❍ Place the mackerel and garlic in a bowl. Pour in half of the cream and add half of the basil. Flake the salmon into another bowl, discarding the skin and any bones. Add the remaining cream and basil to the salmon and season to taste.

❍ Put the salmon mixture in a food processor and process until it forms a rich mousse. Transfer to a bowl and repeat with the mackerel mixture, using a separate bowl.

❍ Bring the stock to the boil in a pan. Remove from the heat and stir in the aspic until completely dissolved. Divide the stock mixture equally between the two mousse mixtures. Set aside.

❍ Line the base and sides of a 900g (2lb) pâté or terrine dish with cling film, then line with the spinach leaves to make the first layer. Add the salmon mousse, pressing down well with the back of a metal spoon. Place the poached pears on top of the salmon mousse. Make a final layer using the mackerel mousse, again pressing down well with the back of a metal spoon. Cover the dish tightly with cling film and chill for 1 hour until the pâté is completely set.

❍ Turn the pâté out of the dish onto a large plate and remove the cling film. Cut the pâté into slices and place 2 slices per person on serving plates. Serve with the endive leaves and the red pepper salsa.

Sardine Ripiene

Stuffed Sardines with Pine Nuts and Spinach

Sardines are under-valued in this country, but it seems that everybody, given the chance and imagination, likes them. My other favourite way of cooking sardines is to bone and cook them in butter until golden, then marinate the cooked sardines in lots of chopped herbs, olive oil and vinegar and store them in the fridge when cold. To make the sardines in this dish easier to eat, remove the heads and tails and butterfly (bone with the fillets still attached at the top) before stuffing (see page 10).

SERVES 4
PREPARATION TIME: 20 MINUTES
COOKING TIME: 10 MINUTES

400g (14oz) spinach, tough stalks removed, then washed
50g (1¾oz) pine nuts, toasted

4 x 175g (6oz) sardines, cleaned
30ml (2 tablespoons) plain flour
2 eggs
30ml (2 tablespoons) chopped fresh flat-leaf parsley
45g (1½oz) unsalted butter
salt and freshly ground black pepper
lemon wedges, to serve

❍ Bring a large pan of water to the boil. Add the spinach and cook for 1 minute until the leaves just wilt. Drain the spinach well in a sieve and squeeze out as much water as possible. Roughly chop the spinach and place in a bowl. Mix in three-quarters of the pine nuts and season to taste.

❍ Fill the fish cavity with the spinach stuffing, then close up the fish. Spread the flour on a flat plate and season with salt and pepper. Dust the fish all over with the seasoned flour.

❍ Beat together the eggs and parsley in a shallow bowl. Heat a non-stick frying pan, then add the butter and heat until frothy. Dip the fish in the egg mixture, turning to coat all over. Place the fish in the pan and cook for 3 minutes on each side over a medium heat until just beginning to brown. Transfer to kitchen paper to drain.

❍ Serve the sardines sprinkled with the remaining pine nuts and garnished with lemon wedges.

Cozze al Peperoncino

Steamed Mussels with Chilli

Mussels are fast food. Once they have been prepared, all the hard work is finished – the dish is cooked and ready on the table in minutes.

I always find that this dish is great for informal gatherings – just bring the pan over to the table and just let everyone help themselves. Provide some rustic Italian bread to mop up the juices from the bottom of the pan.

SERVES 4
PREPARATION TIME: 15 MINUTES
COOKING TIME: 10 MINUTES

2kg (4½lb) mussels, scrubbed clean, beards and barnacles removed
275ml (9fl oz) dry white wine
2 garlic cloves, crushed

8 ripe plum tomatoes, peeled, seeded and chopped (see page 26)
2 fresh red chillies, halved, seeded and chopped
60ml (4 tablespoons) chopped fresh flat-leaf parsley
8 fresh basil leaves, torn
salt and freshly ground black pepper
selection of rustic Italian breads, to serve

❍ Place the mussels and wine in a large heavy-based pan, cover tightly and cook over a high heat, shaking the pan frequently, for 3–5 minutes until the shells have opened. Strain the pan juices through a fine sieve into a bowl. Discard any mussels that have remained closed.

❍ Return both the mussels and pan juices to a clean pan and add the garlic, tomatoes and chilli. Season to taste. Replace the lid, cook for a further 3–4 minutes, shaking the pan occasionally. Add the parsley and basil and shake the pan again. Serve with rustic Italian breads.

Gamberoni in Salsa d'Avocado

Tiger Prawns and Avocado Dip

Prawn and avocado are a traditional combination and can be a bit dated on some menus. However this modern twist, where the prawns are marinated with pink peppercorns, makes the old partnership a winner again.

SERVES 4
PREPARATION TIME: 15 MINUTES
COOKING TIME: 5 MINUTES

2 garlic cloves, finely chopped
1 x 55g (2oz) jar pink peppercorns in oil, drained and roughly chopped
60ml (4 tablespoons) extra virgin olive oil

30g (1oz) fresh coriander
12 raw tiger prawns, heads discarded, peeled with tails left intact and deveined (see page 11)
2 large ripe avocados
15ml (1 tablespoon) mayonnaise
30ml (2 tablespoons) soured cream
sea salt flakes and freshly ground black pepper

❍ Put the garlic, pink peppercorns, 10ml (2 teaspoons) of oil and sea salt in a bowl. Remove half of the coriander leaves from the stalks and finely chop. Stir the chopped coriander into the peppercorn mixture. Add the prawns and marinate for 10 minutes at room temperature.

❍ Meanwhile, using a sharp-bladed knife, cut each avocado in half, cutting around the stone. Twist each half in opposite directions and pull the halves away to separate. Pierce the stone with the side of the knife blade, then twist and lift out the stone. Scoop the flesh into a bowl and mash with a fork. Season to taste, then stir in the mayonnaise and soured cream. Spoon the dip on to 4 serving plates and drizzle with some oil – this will also prevent the avocado from turning brown.

❍ Heat the remaining oil in a frying pan. Lift the prawns from the marinade, shake to drain, then fry them for 2 minutes on each side until bright pink and tender. Remove the prawns from the pan and divide among the plates.

❍ Pour the marinade into the pan juices, bring to the boil and cook for 1 minute. Spoon the marinade over the prawns. Garnish with the remaining coriander sprigs before serving.

Scamponi all'Aglio Affumicato

Grilled Langoustines with Smoked Garlic Butter

There is just no neat way of eating langoustines other than with your hands, but this recipe makes it a bit easier by splitting them down the middle before grilling. Smoked garlic is now widely available in supermarkets – it does give a very distinctive taste to the dish. However, you can use conventional garlic for the garlic butter, if desired.

SERVES 4
PREPARATION TIME: 10 MINUTES
COOKING TIME: 10 MINUTES

12 live langoustines
30ml (2 tablespoons) extra virgin olive oil
170g (6oz) butter
3 fat smoked garlic cloves, crushed

juice of ½ lemon
30ml (2 tablespoons) chopped fresh flat-leaf parsley
salt and freshly ground black pepper

TO SERVE
lemon wedges
crusty bread

❍ Pre-heat the grill to hot.

❍ Bring a large pan of water to the boil. Plunge the live langoustines into the boiling water for 30 seconds until bright pink. Drain, and when cool enough to handle, split in half lengthways. Place the langoustines, cut-side up, on a foil-lined grill pan. Drizzle with olive oil and season to taste.

❍ Place the langoustines under the grill and cook for 5 minutes until chargrilled.

❍ Meanwhile, melt the butter in a frying pan. Add the smoked garlic, lemon juice, parsley and seasoning and cook for 1 minute.

❍ Transfer the langoustines to a large platter and spoon the garlic butter over them. Serve immediately with lemon wedges and crusty bread.

Frittata di Melanzane e Aglefino Affumicato

Aubergine Frittata with Haddock

A *frittata* is an Italian omelette that is cooked either in a pan or baked in the oven. Unlike a French omelette, in which the ingredients are folded inside the eggs, the Italian *frittata* has all of the ingredients mixed with the eggs.

For this *frittata* I've used aubergines, but spinach is also a traditional vegetable used for this dish – just make sure you drain the cooked spinach really well before adding it to the egg mixture. As a variation, I have topped the *frittata* with oak-smoked haddock and garnished it with blanched parsley – delicious!

The *frittata* can be cut into four to serve as a starter, or you can make the portions larger and serve two for a light lunch or supper.

SERVES 4
PREPARATION TIME: 25 MINUTES PLUS
15 MINUTES STANDING
COOKING TIME: 25 MINUTES

1 medium aubergine, trimmed and roughly chopped
2.5ml (½ teaspoon) salt
30ml (2 tablespoons) olive oil
30g (1oz) finely grated fresh Parmesan cheese
55g (2oz) plain flour
30ml (2 tablespoons) chopped fresh chives
2 medium eggs, lightly beaten
15g (½oz) butter
225g (8oz) oak-smoked haddock (if unavailable use undyed smoked haddock)
1 small onion, quartered
1 carrot, halved
1 stick celery, halved
6 whole black peppercorns
30g (1oz) fresh flat-leaf parsley
45ml (3 tablespoons) extra virgin olive oil

❍ Place the chopped aubergine in a colander, sprinkle with the salt and toss to mix. Set the colander on a plate to catch the juices, then leave to stand for 15 minutes. Rinse the aubergines under cold water and pat dry with kitchen paper.

❍ Heat a frying pan until hot. Add the olive oil and, when hot, add the aubergines. Fry for 5–8 minutes until golden brown. Transfer the aubergines to kitchen paper to drain.

❍ Mix together the aubergines, Parmesan cheese, flour and chives in a large bowl. Season to taste. Using a large metal spoon, fold in the beaten eggs.

❍ Heat a heavy-based frying pan until very hot. Add the butter and heat until foaming. Spread the aubergine mixture into the pan. Cook gently for 10–12 minutes until the base is golden brown and the top is just beginning to set.

❍ Meanwhile, place the haddock, skin-side up, and the onion, carrot, celery, peppercorns and 2 sprigs of parsley in a large frying pan. Fill the pan with enough cold water to cover the fish. Gently bring to the boil and cook for 5 minutes. Remove from the heat, cover and leave for 5 minutes until the fish just flakes. Using a fish slice, lift the fish out of the poaching liquid and drain on kitchen paper. Leave until cool enough to handle.

❍ Bring a pan of water to the boil. Holding the remaining parsley by the stalks, plunge it into the water for 30 seconds, then remove and cool under cold water. Remove the leaves from the stalks, pat dry with kitchen paper and roughly chop.

❍ Flake the fish, discarding the skin and bones. Mix together the fish, parsley and 30ml (2 tablespoons) of the extra virgin olive oil. Season to taste.

❍ Pre-heat the grill to hot. Place the frittata under the grill for 2 minutes until the surface is golden brown.

❍ Cut the frittata into 4 and place a wedge on each plate. Spoon over the haddock mixture and drizzle with the remaining extra virgin olive oil. Serve immediately.

Salads

Insalata di Mare

Mixed Seafood Salad

Seafood salad is a fantastic summer dish, but in my restaurants it is popular all the year round served with a Marie-Rose Dressing (see page 170). This one adds peppers and cannellini beans to the mixture for extra colour and crunch, and the dressing gives it a subtle bite. Serve with crusty brown bread.

SERVES 4
PREPARATION TIME: 35 MINUTES PLUS
30 MINUTES SOAKING
COOKING TIME: 10 MINUTES

225g (8oz) mussels
225g (8oz) clams
170g (6oz) piece of firm fish fillet such as cod,
salmon or haddock, skinned and cut
into 1cm (½in) pieces
1 red onion, finely sliced
grated zest and juice of 1 lemon
150ml (5fl oz) dry white wine
4 raw king prawns, peeled and deveined
(see page 11)

225g (8oz), squid, cleaned (see page 12) and cut
into rings
2 x 415g (14½oz) cans cannellini beans, drained,
rinsed and patted dry with kitchen paper
1 red pepper, cored, seeded and finely sliced
1 yellow pepper, cored, seeded and finely sliced
125g (4½oz) peeled prawns
crusty bread, to serve

FOR THE DRESSING
90–120ml (6–8 tablespoons) extra virgin olive oil
30ml (2 tablespoons) red wine vinegar
45ml (3 tablespoons) chopped fresh flat-leaf parsley
1 garlic clove, finely diced
salt and freshly ground black pepper

❍ Scrub the mussels clean and remove the beards and barnacles. Soak the clams in salted water for 30 minutes to remove the grit, then wash in clean water and drain. Steam the fish until tender and just beginning to flake.

❍ Put the onion in a large non-metallic bowl and stir in the lemon zest and juice to keep the onion crisp.

❍ Pour the wine into a deep heavy-based pan. Place the mussels and clams in a steamer basket and put in the pan. Cover tightly and cook for 5 minutes, shaking the pan once. The shellfish are cooked once the shells have opened; discard any that have remained closed. Using a slotted spoon, drain the shellfish and transfer to a large plate. Add the fish. Set aside.

❍ Add the raw prawns and squid to the pan juices and cook for 1–2 minutes until tender. Using a slotted spoon, drain the shellfish and transfer to the plate with the mussels, clams and fish. Bring the pan juices to the boil and cook for 2–3 minutes until reduced to 60ml (4 tablespoons); set aside.

❍ Mix together the cannellini beans and the onion, then stir in the red and yellow peppers and all the shellfish.

❍ In a small bowl, mix together the oil, vinegar, parsley, garlic and reserved pan juices. Season well to taste. Pour the dressing over the shellfish mixture and toss gently. Serve with crusty bread.

Gamberetti Primavera

Shrimp, Apple and Celery Salad

There seems to be great confusion over shrimps and prawns. To me shrimps are smaller than prawns and sweeter in taste too; however, they are that much more fiddly to peel. If you're lucky enough to find live brown shrimps, cook them in a pan of boiling salted water for 5 minutes and serve them with their shells on – eating the shell (head and all) makes them even tastier.

SERVES 4
PREPARATION TIME: 25 MINUTES

450g (1lb) shrimps
3 green dessert apples
juice of 1 lemon
1 head celery, trimmed

1 fennel bulb, trimmed
15ml (1 tablespoon) extra virgin olive oil
30ml (2 tablespoons) Garlic Mayonnaise
(see page 166)
1 head radicchio, trimmed and shredded
salt and freshly ground black pepper
lemon wedges, to serve

❍ Wash the shrimps and drain well. Pat dry with kitchen paper, then remove and discard the shells.

❍ Quarter, core and finely slice the apples, then place them in a large bowl. Add half of the lemon juice and gently coat to prevent the apples from discolouring. Add the shrimps.

❍ Wash the celery and fennel and drain well. Finely chop the celery and finely shred the fennel – add both to the shrimp mixture. Toss to mix.

❍ In a small bowl, mix together the oil, garlic mayonnaise and remaining lemon juice. Season well to taste. Add the dressing to the shrimp mixture and toss gently to mix, adjusting the seasoning, if necessary.

❍ Arrange the shredded radicchio on 4 serving plates and spoon over the shrimp salad. Serve with lemon wedges.

Granchio Tropicale

Tropical Fruit and Crab Salad

This is a very colourful dish. For the best flavour, buy fresh crab meat and use ripe fruit, otherwise this salad will be extremely bland.

Build a good relationship with your fishmonger who can tell you when shellfish such as crabs or lobsters were cooked; don't buy them if they are more than two days old. A fresh cooked crab will smell sweet.

For this recipe I like to use white and brown crab meat as I find the brown meat is the tastiest. Removing all the meat from the crab takes some time and you need to be quite careful keeping the meat shell-free, but it's really worth it!

SERVES 4
PREPARATION TIME: 30 MINUTES

1kg (2¼lb) whole crab, cleaned (see page 11)
30ml (2 tablespoons) extra virgin olive oil
30ml (2 tablespoons) chopped fresh coriander
1 fresh green chilli, seeded and finely chopped
1 large mango, peeled
1 ripe papaya, peeled, halved, seeded and quartered

grated zest and juice of ½ lime
2 kiwi, peeled and quartered lengthways
1 small ripe pineapple, quartered, core removed, then each piece sliced again
salt and freshly ground black pepper

TO SERVE
lime wedges
Quick Guacamole (optional) (see page 168)

○ Remove the brown and white meat from the crab. Gently break the shell of the claws, legs and body part with a meat mallet and carefully remove the meat. Discard the shells. (You should have 250g/9oz crab meat.) Gently stir the oil, coriander and half of the chilli into the crab meat and season to taste with salt and black pepper. Set aside.

○ Holding the mango in the palm of your hand, thinly cut along the length of the stone to give slices.

○ Arrange the mango and papaya slices on a large platter and sprinkle the lime zest and juice over them. Add the kiwi fruit and pineapple wedges to the platter. Spoon the crab meat into the centre and sprinkle with the remaining chilli. Serve with lime wedges and guacamole, if desired.

Tartare di Salmone

Tartare of Salmon with Cucumber and Dill

This recipe calls for wild salmon as the fish needs to be of the freshest and best quality. It's actually made very much like the Swedish *Gravad Lax* except that it's not pressed down or macerated for as long. I've used the word macerate here rather than marinate because the fish is not going to be cooked.

SERVES 4
PREPARATION TIME: 10 MINUTES PLUS
8 HOURS OR OVERNIGHT MACERATING

60ml (4 tablespoons) coarse sea salt
30ml (2 tablespoons) sugar
60ml (4 tablespoons) chopped fresh dill
400g (14oz) wild salmon fillet, skinned, pin-boned
(see page 10) and brown meat removed

salt and freshly ground black pepper
16 sprigs of fresh dill, to garnish

FOR THE SALAD
30ml (2 tablespoons) sunflower oil
5ml (1 teaspoon) white wine vinegar
½ medium cucumber, peeled, halved, seeded and
finely sliced

❍ Mix together the sea salt, sugar and 30ml (2 tablespoons) of chopped dill in a bowl. Place a piece of cling film large enough to completely enclose the salmon on a work surface and sprinkle half of the salt mixture on to it. Place the salmon fillet on top of the salt, then cover the salmon with the remaining salt mixture. Wrap up the salmon like a parcel and leave in the fridge for 8 hours or overnight to macerate.

❍ The next day, wash the salmon in cold water and dry thoroughly with kitchen paper. Cut the salmon into 3mm (⅛in) cubes and place in a clean bowl. Add the remaining 30ml (2 tablespoons) of chopped dill and season to taste. Shape the salmon into 4 patties.

❍ In a bowl, mix together the oil and vinegar. Add the cucumber strips and gently massage them with the dressing for 1–2 minutes. Season to taste.

❍ Place each salmon patty in the centre of a serving plate and surround with the cucumber salad. Garnish with the dill sprigs.

Insalata di Ostriche Calde

Seared Oyster Salad

Raw oysters are not my favourite. However, when they're seared in a pan their flavour and texture is quite fantastic. Here they are used to make a delightful salad – the pecorino shavings adding a very tasty touch.

SERVES 4
PREPARATION TIME: 15 MINUTES
COOKING TIME: 10 MINUTES

170g (6oz) wild rocket or mizuna
1 bunch spring onions, trimmed, shredded and soaked in iced water for 10 minutes
1 cucumber, peeled, halved, seeded and thinly cut into diagonal slices
30ml (2 tablespoons) extra virgin olive oil

55g (2oz) pecorino shavings
24 oysters, shucked
60ml (4 tablespoons) plain flour
60ml (4 tablespoons) cornflour
55g (2oz) butter
15ml (1 tablespoon) chopped fresh rosemary leaves
15ml (1 tablespoon) chopped fresh thyme leaves
30ml (2 tablespoons) fresh lemon juice
salt and freshly ground black pepper

❍ Wash and spin dry the rocket or mizuna, then place in a bowl. Mix in the spring onions and cucumber, drizzle with the oil and season to taste. Arrange in the centre of 4 serving plates and sprinkle over the pecorino cheese shavings.

❍ Pat the oysters dry with kitchen paper. Spread the flour and cornflour on a shallow plate and stir to mix. Season with salt and black pepper. Working in batches, coat the oysters in the seasoned flour.

❍ Heat a heavy-based frying pan until hot. Add the butter and heat until foaming. Working in batches, add the oysters and fry for 5 seconds on each side until golden. Remove from the pan and keep warm while cooking the remaining oysters. Arrange the oysters on the salad.

❍ Add the rosemary and thyme to the pan juices and cook for 30 seconds. Stir in the lemon juice and heat through. Spoon over the oysters and sprinkle with extra black pepper.

Crostini di Pesce

Mixed Seafood Crostini

Crostini are normally topped with a selection of different meats or vegetables. In this recipe I have used three different seafood toppings and they are all equally tasty. Here I have adapted the crostini to make a substantial salad, but they would be quite impressive as party nibbles, too.

SERVES 4
PREPARATION TIME: 30 MINUTES
COOKING TIME: 5 MINUTES

1 ciabatta loaf, cut into 12 (1cm/½in) thick slices
60ml (4 tablespoons) extra virgin olive oil
1 garlic clove, halved
salt and freshly ground black pepper

FOR THE PRAWN TOPPING
30ml (2 tablespoons) mayonnaise (see page 166)
15ml (1 tablespoon) tomato ketchup
15ml (1 tablespoon) lemon juice
a dash of Worcestershire sauce
125g (4½oz) peeled prawns

FOR THE SMOKED SALMON AND TUNA TOPPING
15ml (1 tablespoon) chopped fresh dill
60ml (4 tablespoons) crème fraîche
4 wafer-thin slices smoked salmon
4 wafer-thin slices tuna *carpaccio* (see page 70)

FOR THE CRAB TOPPING
125g (4½oz) fresh crab meat
15ml (1 tablespoon) extra virgin olive oil
15ml (1 tablespoon) chopped fresh coriander leaves
grated zest and juice of ½ lime
50g (1¾oz) finely chopped fresh pineapple

FOR THE SALAD
1 x 225g (8oz) packet prepared mixed salad leaves
125g (4½oz) rocket, washed and drained
60ml (4 tablespoons) extra virgin olive oil
15ml (1 tablespoon) good balsamic vinegar
4 cooked jumbo prawns, to serve

❍ Pre-heat the grill to medium-hot.

❍ Brush the bread slices on both sides with the oil, place on the grill pan and toast until golden brown on both sides. While the bread is still hot, rub both sides with the garlic and sprinkle with black pepper. Set aside.

❍ In a small bowl, mix together the mayonnaise, ketchup, lemon juice and Worcestershire sauce. Stir in the prawns and season to taste. Top 4 crostini with the prawn mixture. Sprinkle with more black pepper.

❍ In another small bowl, mix together the dill and crème fraîche. Spoon the mixture onto 4 crostini. Top each one with a slice of smoked salmon and tuna *carpaccio*.

❍ In another small bowl, mix together the crab meat, oil, coriander, lime zest and juice and pineapple. Season to taste. Top the remaining crostini with the crab mixture.

❍ Place the salad leaves in a large bowl and toss with the oil and vinegar and seasoning. Place the salad on a large platter and arrange the crostini around the edge. Garnish with the jumbo prawns.

❍ For individual servings, divide the salad leaves among 4 large plates and place 3 different crostini in the centre of each. Garnish each serving with a jumbo prawn.

Insalata di Gamberi

Prawn Salad

There are many different types of prawn salad but this one is a personal favourite. I like to keep the shells on as I love the sweet additional flavours they give when cooked. Sometimes I replace the fresh tomatoes with sun-dried tomatoes in oil and add a few toasted pine nuts.

SERVES 4
PREPARATION TIME: 20 MINUTES PLUS
2 HOURS MARINATING
COOKING TIME: 4 MINUTES

1kg (2¼lb) raw tiger prawns
juice of 1 lemon
sea salt
1 large fresh chilli, seeded and finely chopped
2 garlic cloves, finely chopped
120ml (4fl oz) extra virgin olive oil

15g (½oz) fresh basil, stalks removed and leaves torn
1 sprig of fresh parsley, chopped
2 tomatoes, peeled, seeded and diced (see page 26)
1 small red onion, finely diced

TO SERVE
lemon wedges
steamed rice

◯ Remove the heads from the prawns, then peel the shells, leaving the tail end intact. Using a sharp knife, gently cut around the outside curve of each prawn and remove the black vein. To butterfly the prawns, cut all the way through, stopping at the tail but keeping the shells still intact.

◯ Place the prawns in a large shallow dish, making sure to open each one out flat. In a small bowl, mix the lemon juice, sea salt, chilli and garlic. Spoon the mixture over the prawns, then drizzle with the oil. Cover with cling film and leave to marinate in the fridge for 2 hours.

◯ Drain and discard the marinade, then place the prawns, opened out with the tails sticking up, in a large pan. Cook for 2 minutes, shaking the pan occasionally, and then cook for another 2 minutes until the prawns are bright pink.

◯ Place the prawns on a platter and sprinkle with the basil, parsley, tomatoes and onion. Serve with lemon wedges and steamed rice.

Uova in Camicia, Salmone e Asparagi

Poached Egg, Asparagus and Smoked Salmon Salad

This dish is a British classic, with an Italian touch. An alternative, which I also like, is a fillet of poached smoked haddock with an egg on top.
We're all familiar with smoked salmon, but why not try other smoked fish fillets, such as tuna and swordfish, available in good delis and specialist food shops. All are cut into wafer-thin slices just like smoked salmon.

SERVES 4
PREPARATION TIME: 25 MINUTES
COOKING TIME: 15 MINUTES

340g (12oz) asparagus
juice of 2 lemons
1 x 170g (6oz) packet prepared mixed baby salad leaves (such as rocket, spinach, red Swiss chard and little gem)
225g (8oz) smoked salmon
4 free-range eggs

FOR THE DRESSING
60ml (4 tablespoons) extra virgin olive oil
30ml (2 tablespoons) white wine vinegar
1 garlic clove, finely chopped
30ml (2 tablespoons) finely chopped fresh chives
a pinch of sugar
salt and freshly ground black pepper

❍ Trim the 2.5cm (1in) tough end from each asparagus spear, then peel the woody parts to just below the tips with a vegetable peeler.

❍ Fill a tall pan with water and bring to the boil with 1 tablespoon of salt. Stand the asparagus in the pan, stalk-end down, in the water and simmer for 5–8 minutes according to the thickness of the spears. Submerge the tips for the final 2 minutes of cooking, otherwise they will overcook. Drain and submerge the spears in ice-cold water to prevent them from overcooking. Drain and set aside.

❍ Add the lemon juice to a shallow pan of water and bring to a steady simmer.

❍ Meanwhile, place the salad leaves in a large bowl. Mix together the oil, vinegar, garlic, three-quarters of the chives, sugar and seasoning. Pour half of the dressing over the salad leaves and toss to coat. Divide the salad leaves among 4 serving plates. Place the asparagus in the bowl and dress with the remaining oil. Arrange the asparagus on the salad leaves, then top with ruffles of smoked salmon.

❍ Gently crack the eggs into the pan of simmering water and poach for 4–5 minutes. Drain and place a poached egg on top of each salad. Season the eggs well with pepper, sprinkle the remaining chives over them and cut the eggs with a knife just before serving.

Insalata di Razza

Warm Skate Salad

There are numerous ways of preparing and cooking skate. One of my favourites is to cook skate wings very simply in butter and sage and serve with fresh spinach and new potatoes. This time I've opted to poach the skate and serve it with an olive oil and lemon dressing. Remember, never buy skate if there is the slightest hint of an ammonia smell.

SERVES 4
PREPARATION TIME: 30 MINUTES
COOKING TIME: 15 MINUTES

450g (1lb) new season Jersey Royal new potatoes, scrubbed clean
2 x 225g (8oz) skate wings
1 baby fennel, quartered
1 small onion, halved
1 carrot, halved
6 black peppercorns
1 x 100g (3½oz) jar of capers in salt, rinsed and patted dry with kitchen paper

4 thin slices prosciutto, cut into strips
125g (4½oz) baby spinach
125g (4½oz) frisée leaves
125g (4½oz) wild rocket
125g (4½oz) radicchio leaves
60ml (4 tablespoons) extra virgin olive oil
grated zest and juice of 1 lemon
4 tomatoes on the vine, peeled, seeded and cut into wedges (see page 26)
30ml (2 tablespoons) chopped fresh chives
salt and freshly ground black pepper
sunflower oil for deep-frying

❍ Put the potatoes in a deep pan and cover with cold water. Season with salt and bring to the boil. Boil for 10 minutes until tender. Drain.

❍ Meanwhile, place the skate in a large frying pan. Add the fennel, onion, carrot and black peppercorns. Cover with cold water and gently bring to the boil. Remove the pan from the heat, cover tightly and leave for 5 minutes until the fish is tender and flaking.

❍ Pour enough oil for deep-frying into a deep frying pan over a medium heat. Heat until a piece of bread dropped in the oil sizzles and turns golden brown in 30 seconds. Add the capers in batches – they will open out like little flowers. Using a slotted spoon, transfer the capers to kitchen paper to drain. Add the prosciutto to the pan and deep-fry for 1 minute until crisp. Drain on kitchen paper.

❍ Wash and spin dry the salad leaves. Place them in a large bowl and season to taste. Drizzle with 30ml (2 tablespoons) of oil and a little lemon juice. Arrange the salad leaves on 4 large serving plates.

❍ Remove the fish from the poaching liquid and pat dry with kitchen paper. Place the fish on a clean surface and shred with a fork, discarding the cartilage bones.

❍ Mix together the potatoes, tomatoes, chives and half of the capers and prosciutto. Season to taste. Divide among the plates. Top with the shredded skate and drizzle with the remaining oil, lemon zest and juice. Sprinkle the remaining capers and prosciutto over the skate. Serve immediately with plenty of black pepper.

Sgombro Affumicato al Pompelmo

Smoked Mackerel with Grapefruit

This salad is extremely simple and healthy. Mackerel – like tuna – is a fatty fish, but for once this means that it's good for you, being an excellent source of Omega-3 fatty acids. These polyunsaturated fats make the blood less likely to clot, so people who eat these types of fish have a lower risk of heart disease.

SERVES 4
PREPARATION TIME: 10 MINUTES

125g (4½oz) watercress
125g (4½oz) baby spinach
30ml (2 tablespoons) extra virgin olive oil
1 pink grapefruit, peeled and segmented, juice reserved
2 blood oranges, peeled and segmented, juice reserved

280g (10oz) peppered smoked mackerel fillets, skinned
salt and freshly ground black pepper

FOR THE DRESSING
60ml (4 tablespoons) crème fraîche
5ml (1 teaspoon) horseradish sauce
5ml (1 teaspoon) Dijon mustard
15ml (1 tablespoon) chopped fresh flat-leaf parsley
juice of ¼ lemon

❍ Wash and spin dry the watercress and spinach, then place in a bowl. Drizzle with the oil and season to taste. Add the reserved citrus fruit juices. Toss the salad leaves to mix.

❍ Divide the salad among 4 serving plates. Arrange the citrus segments on top. Flake the fish into large pieces and arrange over the salad.

❍ Mix together the crème fraîche, horseradish sauce, mustard, parsley and lemon juice in a small bowl. Season to taste. Drizzle the dressing over the fish before serving.

Carpaccio di Tonno con Rucola e Parmigiano

Tuna Carpaccio with Wild Rocket and Parmesan

Serve this great summer dish with good Italian bread – it makes a perfect healthy lunch that's full of flavour. The tuna needs to be cut very thinly and you may find that freezing it for 1½ hours beforehand will make this easier. When flattening the fish, use the base of a saucepan, as this way the fish is flattened without tearing.

The lemon juice that is spooned on to the flattened fish actually 'cooks' it, so watch for the tuna changing colour as soon as the acid from the lemon hits it.

Try to find wild rocket for the salad – the leaves are much more frilly with fine stems. It also has a stronger peppery taste than the rocket sold in bags in the supermarkets.

SERVES 4
PREPARATION TIME: 15 MINUTES PLUS
1½ HOURS FREEZING

340g (12oz) piece of very fresh tuna fillet
200g (7oz) wild rocket, washed and drained
60ml (4 tablespoons) extra virgin olive oil

15ml (1 tablespoon) fresh lemon juice
55g (2oz) Parmesan cheese shavings
salt and freshly ground black pepper

TO SERVE
lemon wedges
Italian bread

❍ Finely slice the tuna into at least 12 slices. Place 1 slice of tuna between 2 sheets of cling film and bash with the base of a saucepan until very thin. Remove from the cling film and place on a plate. Repeat with remaining tuna, placing 3 pieces on each plate.

❍ Put the rocket into a bowl. Add the oil, lemon juice and seasoning and mix well. Pile the rocket on top of the tuna and sprinkle over the Parmesan cheese shavings. Serve with lemon wedges and Italian bread.

Misto di Verdure all'Aglio e Sarde

Garlic-Grilled Vegetables with Sardines

Fresh sardines are available during the autumn, but you can buy them frozen year-round – look out for them in the chilled cabinet in your supermarket. You should allow two to three large sardines per person, more if smaller. Sardines are great for barbecues – simply scale and clean them and barbecue them whole or filleted; they will make an unusual alternative to the standard fare.

This dish makes the perfect mid-summer lunch or supper, accompanied with a chilled glass of Prosecco – just the job for a hot day!

SERVES 4
PREPARATION TIME: 35 MINUTES
COOKING TIME: 35–45 MINUTES

1 red pepper, cored and seeded
1 yellow pepper, cored and seeded
1 large carrot
2 large courgettes, trimmed
1 medium aubergine, trimmed
2 heads chicory, trimmed
90ml (6 tablespoons) extra virgin olive oil
1 x 200g (7oz) jar artichoke hearts in oil, drained

3 garlic cloves, finely chopped
60ml (4 tablespoons) finely chopped fresh rosemary leaves
90ml (6 tablespoons) finely chopped fresh flat-leaf parsley
45ml (3 tablespoons) finely chopped fresh basil
30ml (2 tablespoons) plain flour
900g (2lb) sardines, cleaned and filleted
salt and freshly ground black pepper
extra virgin olive oil, to serve

❍ Pre-heat the grill to medium-hot.

❍ Put the red and yellow peppers, skin-side up, on a grill pan and grill for 5–8 minutes until the skins are blackened. Transfer to a bowl, cover with cling film and allow to cool for 5 minutes. Peel off the skins and discard. Set aside.

❍ Meanwhile, place the carrot in a pan of water and bring to the boil. Cook for 5 minutes until just tender when gently pressed. Drain, and when cool enough to handle, thinly slice lengthways. Thinly slice the courgettes and aubergine lengthways and quarter the chicory.

❍ Line a large grill pan with foil and place the carrot, courgettes, aubergine and chicory on top. Drizzle with 15ml (1 tablespoon) extra virgin olive oil and grill for 8–10 minutes until the vegetables are tender and just beginning to brown in places. Transfer the grilled vegetables to a large shallow dish. (You may need to grill the vegetables in 2 batches if your grill pan is small. In that case, keep the first batch warm while the second batch is cooking.) Add the red and yellow peppers and the drained artichoke hearts to the grilled vegetables.

❍ In a small bowl, mix together the garlic, rosemary, parsley, basil and 45ml (3 tablespoons) extra virgin olive oil. Season with salt and pepper. Pour the dressing over the grilled vegetables while they are still warm and set aside for 10 minutes.

❍ Spread the flour on a flat plate and season with salt and black pepper. Coat the sardine fillets in the seasoned flour. Heat the remaining olive oil in a non-stick frying pan and add the sardines. Fry over a medium heat for 3–4 minutes on both sides until golden brown. Drain on kitchen paper.

❍ Lift the vegetables from the dressing and arrange around the edge of a large serving platter; place the sardines in the centre. Sprinkle with the dressing and a little more extra virgin olive oil before serving.

Pasta, Pizza & Risotto

Pappardelle ai Gamberi con Verdure

Pappardelle with Prawns and Vegetables

Tiger prawns are easily recognized by the striped markings across their back, which are visible when they're raw. Orangey-grey in colour, they turn pink when cooked. They're now widely available raw in fishmongers and supermarkets, especially in the frozen section, and also in oriental supermarkets. As an alternative you can use the large Mediterranean prawns.

Pappardelle are wide pasta ribbons frequently used in Tuscan cooking. In Italy, each pasta has a special sauce associated with it, and this very chunky sauce is a great example.

SERVES 4
PREPARATION TIME: 20 MINUTES
COOKING TIME: 12–14 MINUTES

30ml (2 tablespoons) vegetable oil
2 garlic cloves, finely diced
1 red pepper, halved lengthways, seeded and cut into long batons
1 yellow pepper, halved lengthways, seeded and cut into long batons
1 courgette, trimmed and cut into matchsticks
75ml (2½fl oz) white wine
1 x 400g (14oz) can whole peeled plum tomatoes
15ml (1 tablespoon) olive oil
32–40 raw tiger prawns, heads discarded, peeled and deveined (see page 11)
60–75ml (4–5 tablespoons) fresh basil leaves
30ml (2 tablespoons) chopped fresh flat-leaf parsley
250g (9oz) pappardelle
salt and freshly ground black pepper

❍ Bring a large pan of salted water to a rolling boil.

❍ Heat the vegetable oil in a large pan over a medium heat. Add the garlic and cook for 1 minute until golden brown. Stir in the red and yellow peppers and cook for a further 3–4 minutes. Stir in the courgette and cook for 1 minute more.

❍ Stir the wine into the vegetables and bring to a boil. Cook for 3–4 minutes until the alcohol evaporates. Place the tomatoes in a food processor and process until roughly chopped. Stir the purée into the vegetables and cook for 2 minutes.

❍ Heat the olive oil in a small pan over a medium heat. Add the prawns and cook, stirring, for 1–2 minutes until heated through. Add the prawns, pan juices, basil and parsley to the tomato mixture. Season to taste.

❍ Meanwhile, add the pasta to the pan of boiling water and return to a rolling boil. Stir and cook for 5–7 minutes until al dente. Drain, add to the vegetable mixture and toss well. Serve immediately with extra black pepper.

Linguine alle Acciughe

Linguine with Anchovies

Preserved anchovies are not greatly used in the UK despite the fact that there are many different varieties available. Supermarkets stock anchovies loose in olive oil and they are also sold in cans or jars. Good delis sell fresh marinated anchovies and these are my favourite type for this recipe. You can also find anchovies preserved in salt – they're extremely strong in flavour and need to be soaked in milk before using.

SERVES 4
COOKING TIME: 20 MINUTES
PREPARATION TIME: 15–20 MINUTES

340g (12oz) linguine
15g (^{1}/$_2$oz) fresh basil leaves
60ml (4 tablespoons) chopped fresh flat-leaf parsley
salt and freshly ground black pepper

FOR THE SAUCE
60ml (4 tablespoons) olive oil
2 garlic cloves, crushed
3 spring onions, trimmed and finely chopped
1 x 125g (4^1/$_2$oz) jar sun-dried tomatoes in oil, drained and finely chopped
6 anchovy fillets in olive oil, drained and finely chopped
150ml (5fl oz) white wine
150ml (5fl oz) Fish Stock (see page 164)

❍ Bring a large pan of salted water to a rolling boil.

❍ Heat half of the oil in a large frying pan over a medium heat. Add the garlic, spring onions, sun-dried tomatoes and anchovies. Stir well and gently fry for 3–5 minutes until the onions are golden.

❍ Stir the wine and stock into the onion mixture and bring to the boil. Reduce the heat to a simmer and cook for 10 minutes.

❍ Meanwhile, add the pasta to the pan of boiling water and return to a rolling boil. Stir and cook for 8–10 minutes until al dente. Drain, reserving 150ml (5fl oz) of the cooking liquid.

❍ Add the linguine and the remaining oil to the sauce and toss them together over a low heat. Add some of the reserved cooking liquid if the mixture is a little dry. Stir in the basil and parsley and season to taste. Serve immediately.

Risotto di Gamberi Scampi con Spinaci e Zafferano

Prawn, Spinach and Saffron Risotto

The secret to a good seafood risotto is always to have a well-flavoured stock, so if you can find the time, I would suggest making it yourself.

I often like to use fish and vegetables together and spinach is one of my favourite vegetables. If you are not a great fan of spinach, you can replace it with a vegetable such as courgettes.

The saffron adds a delicate taste and excellent colour for presentation. .

SERVES 4
PREPARATION TIME: 30 MINUTES
COOKING TIME: 30 MINUTES

15ml (1 tablespoon) vegetable oil
1 medium onion, finely diced
1 bay leaf
150ml (5fl oz) white wine
1.5 litres (2¾ pints) Fish Stock (see page 164)

4 langoustines
340g (12oz) risotto rice
a good pinch of saffron strands
340g (12oz) peeled prawns
225g (8oz) baby spinach, washed and drained
8 fresh basil leaves
55g (2oz) butter
1 garlic clove, sliced

❍ Heat the oil in a large pan over a medium heat. Add the onion and bay leaf and cook over a gentle heat for 3–4 minutes until the onion is soft.

❍ Meanwhile, place the wine and a little stock in a separate pan and bring to the boil. Add the langoustines, cover and cook for 2–3 minutes until bright pink. Drain, setting aside the langoustines and reserving the pan juices.

❍ Stir the rice into the onion mixture, then add the saffron and reserved pan juices. Stir and simmer for about 5 minutes until the liquid is absorbed.

❍ Meanwhile, pour the remaining stock into a large pan and allow to gently simmer. Gradually add the stock, a ladleful at a time, to the rice, stirring and adding more stock as each batch is absorbed. The total cooking time will be about 20 minutes, at the end of which the rice should be al dente. Season well to taste.

❍ Add the prawns, spinach and basil leaves to the risotto and cook for 2–3 minutes – the spinach should just be wilted.

❍ Meanwhile, melt the butter in a small frying pan and add the garlic. Cook for 1 minute, then add the langoustines. Cook for 1 minute to heat through. Remove the langoustines and set aside. Stir the melted butter into the risotto.

❍ Spoon the risotto into large warmed serving bowls and garnish with the langoustines.

Gnocchi Mare e Pesto

Seafood Gnocchi and Pesto Sauce

When I was growing up in Italy, this would have been regarded as 'poor man's food'.
It makes a great family dish.
If you don't have time to make your own gnocchi, you can buy it in supermarkets – the
varieties available are very good.

SERVES 4
PREPARATION TIME: 20 MINUTES PLUS
30 MINUTES SOAKING
COOKING TIME: 15 MINUTES

200g (7oz) mussels
200g (7oz) clams
45g (1½oz) fresh basil, stalks discarded
30g (1oz) fresh flat-leaf parsley

3 garlic cloves, crushed
55g (2oz) pine nuts
30g (1oz) freshly grated pecorino cheese
15ml (1 tablespoon) salt
5ml (1 teaspoon) freshly ground black pepper
120ml (8 tablespoons) olive oil
4 langoustines
150ml (5fl oz) white wine
450g (1lb) Gnocchi (see page 174)

❍ Scrub the mussels clean and remove the beards and barnacles. Soak the clams in salted water for 30 minutes to remove the grit, then wash in clean water and drain.

❍ Bring a large pan of salted water to a rolling boil.

❍ Put the basil, parsley, two-thirds of the garlic, pine nuts, pecorino cheese, salt, black pepper and half of the oil into a food processor. Process until the texture is like coarse breadcrumbs. Adjust the amount of oil you use accordingly.

❍ Heat a little oil in a deep heavy-based pan, add the remaining garlic, then the mussels and the clams. Cover tightly and cook over a gentle heat for 3–5 minutes, shaking the pan frequently, until the shells have opened. Discard any shellfish that has remained closed. Add the langoustines and wine and simmer over a low heat for 5 minutes.

❍ Add the gnocchi to the boiling water and return to a rolling boil. Stir and cook for 2–3 minutes until they rise to the surface, then cook for another 30 seconds until al dente. Drain.

❍ Add the gnocchi, pesto sauce and a little extra oil to the shellfish. If the clams or mussels fall out of their shells, simply discard the shells. Serve immediately.

Fettuccine al Salmone e Grappa

Smoked Salmon, Grappa and Truffle Fettuccine

Truffle oil is a good investment. Because it has a very intense flavour, a little goes a long way. It can be drizzled on salads, vegetables (try it in mashed potatoes), pasta, risotto, seafood and meat. When buying, be sure that the oil is 'fresh' as it does tend to lose its pungency about a year after manufacture.

SERVES 4
PREPARATION TIME: 20 MINUTES
COOKING TIME: 15 MINUTES

55g (2oz) butter
1 large leek, trimmed and finely chopped
225g (8oz) smoked salmon strips
1 shot of grappa

300ml (10fl oz) béchamel sauce (see page 94)
freshly grated nutmeg
340g (12oz) fettuccine
300ml (10fl oz) double cream
15ml (1 tablespoon) white truffle oil
15ml (1 tablespoon) chopped fresh coriander
salt and freshly ground black pepper

❍ Bring a large pan of salted water to a rolling boil.

❍ Meanwhile, melt the butter in a large frying pan, add the leek and cook over a gentle heat for 5–8 minutes until soft and just beginning to turn golden. Add the salmon. Put the grappa into a large metal ladle and ignite, then add to the salmon mixture. Once the flames die down, stir in the béchamel sauce and cook, stirring gently, for 5 minutes. Season to taste with the salt, black pepper and nutmeg. Remove the frying pan from the heat and set aside.

❍ Meanwhile, add the pasta to the pan of boiling water and return to the boil. Stir and cook for 3–5 minutes until al dente. Drain, reserving 150ml (5fl oz) of the cooking liquid.

❍ Add the pasta to the salmon sauce, then stir in the cream, truffle oil and coriander, tossing them together. Continue to cook for 1–2 minutes until well tossed and the cream is heated through. Add some of the reserved cooking liquid if the mixture is a little dry. Serve immediately with plenty of freshly ground black pepper.

Tagliatelle al Salmone e Asparagi

Tagliatelle with Salmon and Asparagus

This is one of the first dishes that I cooked in Zilli Fish for a small party. Salmon and asparagus are a classic combination and here the flavours blend especially beautifully. It must be popular because it's still on the menu today.
A little warning: this dish is quite rich and makes a filling main course, but it will also serve six as a starter.

SERVES 4–6
COOKING TIME: 25 MINUTES
PREPARATION TIME: 20 MINUTES

8 jumbo asparagus spears or 16 thin asparagus
280g (10oz) salmon fillet, thinly sliced
15ml (1 tablespoon) butter
2 garlic cloves, crushed
75ml (3fl oz) Fish Stock (see page 164)
275ml (9fl oz) single cream
340g (12oz) tagliatelle
5ml (1 teaspoon) oil

15g (½oz) chopped fresh flat-leaf parsley
15g (½oz) chopped fresh dill
15ml (1 tablespoon) Pernod
4 thin fillets smoked salmon
salt and freshly ground black pepper
fresh dill sprigs, to garnish
15g (½oz) fresh basil leaves, torn, to garnish

❍ Bring 2 large pans of salted water to a rolling boil.

❍ If you are using the jumbo asparagus, trim the 2.5cm (1in) tough end from each spear, then peel the woody parts to just below the tips with a vegetable peeler.

❍ Blanch the asparagus in one of the pans of boiling water for 1–2 minutes until al dente. Drain and chop the asparagus into 1cm (½in) pieces, leaving the tips whole.

❍ Reserve 4 of the salmon fillet slices and cut the remainder into small cubes.

❍ Heat a large frying pan over a medium heat, add the butter and heat until melted. Add the garlic and

fry for 1 minute until golden brown. Stir in the asparagus and the salmon pieces and cook for 3 minutes until the salmon is just tender. Using a slotted spoon, transfer the fish and asparagus to a plate. Set aside.

❍ Pour the stock and cream into the pan juices and bring to a gentle simmer. Cook over a low heat for 8–10 minutes.

❍ Meanwhile, add the pasta to the second pan of boiling water and return to a rolling boil. Stir and cook for 3–5 minutes until al dente. Drain, reserving 150ml (5fl oz) of the cooking liquid.

❍ Add the pasta to the cream sauce and toss gently over a low heat. Add some of the reserved cooking liquid if the mixture is little dry. Return the asparagus and the salmon pieces to the pan and season well to taste. Stir gently to mix and cook for a further 3 minutes.

❍ Meanwhile, pre-heat a ridged cast-iron grill pan on the hob until smoking. Brush the reserved salmon fillet slices with the oil and place on the grill pan. Cook for 1 minute, then turn the fish 45 degrees and cook for 1 minute. Turn the fish over and repeat; you should have criss-cross lines on both sides.

❍ Stir the parsley, dill and Pernod into the pasta, then place it in the centre of 4 warmed plates. Wrap a piece of the smoked salmon around one side of each mound of pasta, then place a piece of the reserved salmon fillet to one side. Spoon any remaining sauce over the salmon. Garnish with the dill sprigs and serve immediately.

Risotto di Mare

Seafood Risotto

The selection of fish used in this risotto is very much up to you. Use firm white fish — cod and/or salmon are the best – as they will not break up as easily as the more delicate varieties such as sea bass or red mullet. For the shellfish, clams and prawns are also good as are squid rings and tentacles.

Leftover risotto makes excellent risotto cakes – just remove and discard any shells from the shellfish. Gather the mixture to make large patties and then cover in flour, beaten egg and dried breadcrumbs. Cook in a little butter, then bake until golden brown all over and heated through. Serve with a light salad.

SERVES 4
PREPARATION TIME: 30 MINUTES
COOKING TIME: 30 MINUTES

1.5 litres (2¾ pints) Fish Stock (see page 164)
85g (3oz) butter
1 medium onion, finely diced
2 garlic cloves, finely diced
1 bay leaf, torn in half

340g (12oz) risotto rice
225g (8oz) mussels, scrubbed clean, beards and barnacles removed
150ml (5fl oz) white wine such as Prosecco
170g (6oz) firm fish fillet such as cod, salmon or haddock, skinned and cut into 5cm (2in) pieces
30ml (2 tablespoons) chopped fresh parsley
15ml (1 tablespoon) chopped fresh chives
salt and freshly ground black pepper

○ Pour the stock into a large pan and bring to a gentle simmer.

○ Melt 30g (1oz) of the butter in a large pan, add the onion, garlic, and 2 bay leaf halves and sauté for 5–8 minutes until soft. Stir in the rice. Cook, stirring, for about 30 seconds.

○ Gradually add the stock, a ladleful at a time, to the rice, stirring and adding more stock as each batch is absorbed. The total cooking time will be about 20 minutes, at the end of which the rice should be al dente. Season well to taste. Set aside.

○ Meanwhile, place the mussels in a separate pan, add the wine, cover tightly and cook over a high heat for 3–5 minutes, shaking the pan frequently, until the shells have opened. Strain the pan juices through a fine sieve and reserve. Discard any mussels that have remained closed.

○ Return the risotto to a low heat and stir in the remaining butter. Add some of the reserved pan juices if the risotto is a little dry. Stir in the fish, parsley and chives and season to taste. Cook for a further 1–2 minutes until the fish is tender and just flakes. Discard the bay leaf halves.

○ Spoon the risotto into 4 large warmed bowls and arrange the mussels around the edge. Sprinkle with extra black pepper and serve immediately.

Spaghetti alle Vongole in Pomodoro

Spaghetti with Clams and Baby Plum Tomatoes

I sometimes make this dish without the tomatoes but this version is my favourite. Look out for baby plum tomatoes or, if available, organic tomatoes which give a much better flavour.

SERVES 4
PREPARATION TIME: 20 MINUTES PLUS
30 MINUTES SOAKING
COOKING TIME: 15 MINUTES

340g (12oz) clams
3 fat garlic cloves
120ml (4fl oz) olive oil
1 fresh red chilli

4 bay leaves
120ml (4fl oz) good white wine
450g (1lb) baby plum tomatoes,
halved lengthways
30g (1oz) fresh basil, stalks discarded
30g (1oz) fresh flat-leaf parsley, finely chopped
450g (1lb) spaghetti
salt and freshly ground black pepper
extra virgin olive oil, to drizzle

❍ Soak the clams in salted water for 30 minutes to remove the grit, then wash in clean water and drain.

❍ Bring a large pan of salted water to a rolling boil.

❍ Place the unpeeled garlic cloves on a clean surface and crush with the blade of a heavy knife. Put the oil in a large non-stick frying pan and add the garlic, chilli and bay leaves. Cook for 1 minute over a low heat. Add the clams, cover and cook for 2–3 minutes. Once opened, pour in the wine and simmer for 3 minutes over a medium heat. Add the tomatoes, basil and parsley and cook for a further 5 minutes over a low heat. Set aside.

❍ Meanwhile, ease the pasta into the pan of boiling water and return to a rolling boil. Stir and cook for 5–8 minutes until al dente. Drain.

❍ Place the pasta in a large bowl and pour the clam sauce over it. If you find there are two many shells, remove and discard some of them, and also discard the whole chilli. Drizzle with extra virgin olive oil and toss to mix. Adjust the seasoning and serve immediately.

Ravioli di Aragosta

Lobster Ravioli

Enzo is one of my pasta chefs at Zilli Fish and he really does make rather good ravioli. Because he originates from the same region in Italy as I do, the flavours and taste of his food often take me back to my younger days. This is a great recipe for one of your own nostalgic days or for a party!

When rolling out the pasta, a pasta machine really makes life simple – it's almost impossible to roll it out as thinly as required with a rolling pin. Home-made pasta tastes so delicate and fresh – you have to try it to see. Use the dough immediately after making it.

SERVES 4
PREPARATION TIME: 45 MINUTES PLUS
30 MINUTES RESTING
COOKING TIME: 45 MINUTES

FOR THE RAVIOLI DOUGH
400g (14oz) 00 flour
4 eggs
30ml (2 tablespoons) olive oil
a pinch of salt
75ml (5 tablespoons) cold water
extra flour for dusting

FOR THE LOBSTER FILLING
2 x 450g (1lb) lobsters, cooked (see page 11),
shelled (reserve the shells and pound them)
and the meat finely chopped
60ml (4 tablespoons) mascarpone
15ml (1 tablespoon) chopped fresh flat-leaf parsley
6 fresh basil leaves, shredded

FOR THE LOBSTER SAUCE
45ml (3 tablespoons) olive oil
30g (1oz) butter
1 small onion, finely chopped
1 stick celery, trimmed and finely chopped
1 small carrot, finely chopped
1 fat garlic clove, crushed
30g (1oz) plain flour
15ml (1 tablespoon) tomato purée
60ml (2fl oz) brandy
300ml (10fl oz) good Fish Stock (see page 164)
600ml (1 pint) double cream
salt and freshly ground black pepper

◯ Put the flour on a work surface, make a well in the centre and add the eggs, oil and salt. Using your fingers in a circular motion, slowly incorporate the flour into the egg mixture. Add the water if required to form a dough. Knead for 5 minutes, adding extra flour to the surface, if necessary, until the dough is elastic and springs back when gently pressed. Cover with cling film and allow to rest for 30 minutes.

◯ Meanwhile, mix all the filling ingredients together and season to taste. Set aside.

❍ Heat the oil in a heavy-based pan, add the butter and heat until melted. Stir in the onion, celery, carrot and garlic and cook over a very low heat for 10 minutes until soft. Add the pounded lobster shells, flour and tomato purée and cook, stirring well, for a further 5 minutes.

❍ Put the brandy in a large metal ladle or small pan and ignite, then pour over the vegetables. Once the flames die down, stir in the stock and cream. Cook over a low heat for 20 minutes until reduced to a coating consistency. Pass the sauce through a fine sieve, then return it to a clean pan. Season to taste and set aside.

❍ Fill the ravioli while the sauce is cooking. Using a pasta machine, roll out all the pasta dough on a floured surface, fold over lengthways in half, mark a point at the crease and unfold again. Using a piping bag with a plain nozzle, pipe the lobster filling mixture on to one-half of the pasta at 2.5cm (1in) intervals, fold over the other leaf of pasta and seal around the filling using your fingertips. Cut out the ravioli either in squares or by using a round pastry cutter; crimp the edges with a fork.

❍ Bring a large pan of salted water to a rolling boil. Add the lobster ravioli in batches. Once the ravioli rise to the surface, cook for 1 minute more, drain and place in the pan of hot lobster sauce. Shake the pan gently to coat the ravioli with the sauce and serve immediately.

Risotto al Nero di Seppie e Capesante

Black Ink Risotto and Scallops

Black risotto is somewhat trendy at the moment, but I remember as a child that it was the cheapest dish my mother could make for a large family meal. If you can buy fresh cuttlefish and take out the ink yourself it is much better than getting the sachets from the fishmongers. The sachets of ink come in 5ml (1 teaspoon) packets; it may not sound like much, but this is enough to flavour and colour at least 225g (8oz) pasta or 340g (12oz) risotto rice. The ink, which has a 'fishy' flavour, is very thick, and stains easily.

SERVES 4
PREPARATION TIME: 25 MINUTES
COOKING TIME: 35 MINUTES

1.5 litre (2¾ pints) Fish Stock (see page 164)
55g (2oz) butter
1 red onion, diced
2 bay leaves
1 sprig of fresh thyme
340g (12oz) risotto rice

1 x 5ml (1 teaspoon) sachet of
cuttlefish or squid ink
150ml (5fl oz) white wine
1 red pepper, roasted, seeded and finely diced
16 king scallops, corals detached and finely
chopped, washed and patted dry
30ml (2 tablespoons) roughly chopped fresh
flat-leaf parsley
90ml (6 tablespoons) extra virgin olive oil
salt and freshly ground black pepper

○ Pour the stock into a large pan and bring to a gentle simmer.

○ Melt the butter in a large heavy-based pan, add the onion, bay leaves and thyme and cook for 3–5 minutes until the onion is soft. Add the rice and squid ink and stir for 1 minute over a medium heat. Add the wine and cook for a further 5–7 minutes until it is absorbed.

○ Reserve 2 ladles of stock, then gradually add the remainder, a ladleful at a time, to the rice, stirring and adding more stock as each batch is absorbed. The total cooking time will be about 20 minutes, at the end of which the rice should be al dente. Stir in the chopped scallop corals. Set aside.

○ Slice the pepper into thin strips and mix with the parsley and 60ml (4 tablespoons) of the oil.

○ Heat another 15–30ml (1–2 tablespoons) oil in a heavy-based frying pan and stir-fry the scallops for 1–2 minutes until they are just tinged golden on the outside. If the scallops are very thick, slice them through the middle.

○ Return the risotto to a low heat and stir in the remaining stock. Remove and discard the bay leaves and thyme sprig. Season well to taste.

○ Spoon the risotto onto 4 warmed serving plates, then top with the scallops and the roasted pepper strips. Serve immediately.

Pasta con Patate e Cozze

Pasta with Potatoes and Mussels

This was my father's favourite recipe, purely because it was easy and cheap to make for the family on a Sunday when my mother was resting. The pasta and potato combination was my father's own idea, and the dish was very filling.

SERVES 4
PREPARATION TIME: 15 MINUTES
COOKING TIME: 25 MINUTES

600g (1lb 5oz) mussels, scrubbed clean, beards and barnacles removed
75ml (5 tablespoons) water

105ml (7 tablespoons) extra virgin olive oil
1 garlic clove, crushed
450g (1lb) starchy potatoes such as Romano, peeled and cut into small cubes
250g (9oz) short rigid pasta, such as baby macaroni
15g (½oz) fresh flat-leaf parsley, stalks discarded
salt and freshly ground black pepper

❍ Place the mussels and water in a large heavy-based pan, cover tightly and cook over a high heat for 3–5 minutes, shaking the pan frequently until the shells have opened.

❍ Strain the pan juices through a fine sieve into a bowl and reserve. Discard any mussels that have remained closed. Remove the mussels from their shells and set aside.

❍ Meanwhile, bring a large pan of salted water to a rolling boil.

❍ Heat the oil in a large frying pan, add the garlic and cook for 2 minutes until brown. Remove and discard the garlic. Add the potatoes to the pan and cook for 8–10 minutes until tender and just golden. Stir in the mussels and season with salt to taste.

❍ Add the pasta to the pan of boiling water and return to a rolling boil. Stir the pasta and cook for 8–10 minutes until al dente, then drain. Add the pasta, the reserved pan juices and the parsley to the mussel mixture and toss to mix. Season to taste and serve immediately.

Fusilli Scoglio

Fusilli with Shellfish Sauce

Kid's love this twirl-shaped pasta. It has made a comeback and is now becoming a trendy pasta. For a spicier dish, add a chopped fresh red chilli.

SERVES 4
PREPARATION TIME: 30 MINUTES PLUS
30 MINUTES SOAKING
COOKING TIME: 20 MINUTES

340g (12oz) fusilli or pasta twists
salt and freshly ground black pepper
sprigs of fresh flat-leaf parsley, to garnish

FOR THE SAUCE
450g (1lb) mussels
450g (1lb) clams
60ml (4 tablespoons) extra virgin olive oil
75ml (5 tablespoons) water
3 garlic cloves, chopped
200g (7oz) queen scallops, washed and patted dry
30ml (2 tablespoons) chopped fresh flat-leaf parsley
4 plum tomatoes, peeled, seeded and chopped
(see page 26)

❍ Scrub the mussels clean and remove the beards and barnacles. Soak the clams in salted water for 30 minutes to remove the grit, then wash in clean water and drain.

❍ Bring a large pan of salted water to a rolling boil.

❍ Heat half of the oil in a large heavy-based pan. Place the mussels, clams and 75ml (5 tablespoons) of water in the pan, cover tightly and cook over a high heat for 3–5 minutes, shaking the pan frequently, until the shells are open.

❍ Strain the pan juices through a fine sieve into a bowl and reserve. Remove the shells from the mussels and clams, discarding any shellfish that have remained closed.

❍ Heat the remaining oil in the pan, add the garlic and cook for 1 minute until golden. Add the scallops and stir-fry for 1–2 minutes until just tinged golden on the outside. Return the pan juices and shellfish to the pan. Stir in the parsley and tomatoes. Season well to taste. Remove the pan from the heat.

❍ Add the pasta to the pan of boiling water and return to a rolling boil. Stir and cook for 10 minutes until al dente. Drain, reserving 150ml (5fl oz) of the cooking liquid. Add the pasta to the shellfish and toss to mix. Add some of the reserved cooking liquid if the mixture is a little dry. Garnish with sprigs of flat-leaf parsley and serve immediately.

Crespelle ai Frutti di Mare

Seafood Crêpes

These crêpes have been kept light with a simple filling of béchamel sauce and mixed seafood; no extra sauce is served on top, just a good drizzling of extra virgin olive oil. A light mixed salad of your choosing will complete the meal. This is a great recipe for using up small quantities of leftover fish.

These days, the mixed packets of prepared salads in supermarkets are getting more and more adventurous – the one used here included frisée with red Swiss chard and fine sticks of crispy raw beetroot; I couldn't have made it better myself!

SERVES 4
PREPARATION TIME: 35 MINUTES
COOKING TIME: 40 MINUTES

FOR THE CRÊPE BATTER
55g (2oz) plain flour
1 egg, lightly beaten
300ml (10fl oz) milk
a pinch of salt
30g (1oz) butter, melted
15ml (1 tablespoon) chopped fresh flat-leaf parsley
extra virgin olive oil, to drizzle

FOR THE BÉCHAMEL SAUCE
15g ($\frac{1}{2}$oz) butter
15g ($\frac{1}{2}$oz) plain flour
150ml (5fl oz) milk
a pinch of ground nutmeg
5ml (1 teaspoon) English mustard
55g (2oz) gruyère cheese, grated
150ml (5fl oz) double cream, lightly whipped

FOR THE FILLING
125g (4$\frac{1}{2}$oz) cod fillet
55g (2oz) salmon fillet
55g (2oz) peeled cooked prawns
170g (6oz) mussels, scrubbed clean, beards and barnacles removed, cooked and shelled
salt and freshly ground black pepper

TO SERVE
1 x 200g (7oz) packet of prepared mixed salad leaves

○ To make the batter, place the flour, egg, milk and salt in a food processor or blender and process for 2 minutes. Add the melted butter and parsley and process for a further 20 seconds. Pour the mixture into a jug and allow to stand for at least 10 minutes before using.

○ Meanwhile, to make the sauce, melt the butter in a heavy-based pan. Add the flour and cook for 1 minute. Gradually add the milk, stirring continuously, until the sauce is smooth. Stir in the nutmeg and mustard and cook for a further 8 minutes. Remove from the heat. Add the gruyère cheese, stir until melted, then fold in the cream. Set aside.

❍ Lightly grease a non-stick crêpe pan and set over a high heat. Ladle in enough batter to lightly coat the base. Cook for 1–2 minutes until the batter changes colour and the edges brown, then flip the crêpe over and cook for 1 minute. Remove from the pan and continue to make 8 crêpes in total. Layer the crêpes between sheets of greaseproof paper and keep warm.

❍ Pre-heat the oven to 220°C/425°F/Gas Mark 7.

❍ Bring a pan of salted water to the boil. Be sure that all the fish are free from skin and bone, then dice the uncooked fish and plunge into boiling water for 30 seconds. Drain and pat dry with kitchen paper. Mix all of the seafood and the sauce together in a large bowl. Season to taste.

❍ Divide the filling among the crêpes, keeping it on a quarter of the crêpe. Fold the crêpes into quarters and place on a baking tray; drizzle with a little extra virgin olive oil. Bake for 10 minutes until the crêpes just begin to crisp.

❍ Cut each crêpe into 2 or 4 pieces and arrange on large serving plates. Place the salad close to the crêpes, then drizzle with a little more oil. Sprinkle with black pepper and serve immediately.

Capelli d'Angelo al Tonno

Angel Hair Pasta with Tuna

My assistant chef, Andy Campbell, and I came up with this recipe while cooking on GMTV. It worked so well that it's now a regular on my menu. Angel hair pasta is the finest of all the long pastas. It's perfect served in a light fish or vegetable sauce.

SERVES 4
PREPARATION TIME: 35 MINUTES PLUS
30 MINUTES INFUSING
COOKING TIME: 35 MINUTES

FOR THE TUNA
600ml (1 pint) sunflower oil
6 garlic cloves, peeled
4 sprigs of fresh rosemary
4 bay leaves
4 sprigs of fresh thyme
10 black peppercorns
4 strips of lemon zest
450g (1lb) fresh tuna, cut into 5cm (2in) cubes

FOR THE ROASTED PEPPERS
4 yellow peppers, halved lengthways and seeded
1 garlic clove, finely diced
30ml (2 tablespoons) extra virgin olive oil
15ml (1 tablespoon) balsamic vinegar
sea salt and freshly ground black pepper

FOR THE PASTA
225g (8oz) angel hair pasta
2 beef tomatoes, peeled, seeded and roughly chopped (see page 26)
2 small dried chillies, crumbled
30ml (2 tablespoons) extra virgin olive oil
10 fresh basil leaves, roughly torn
extra virgin olive oil, to drizzle

○ Pour the sunflower oil into a deep pan and place a cooking thermometer into the oil. Add the garlic, rosemary, bay leaves, thyme, black peppercorns and lemon zest. Heat gently to 80°C–100°C (176°F–212°F) and allow to infuse at this temperature for 20–30 minutes.

○ Gently add the tuna to the oil. As soon as the tuna starts to colour, remove the pan from the heat and allow the oil to cool before removing the tuna. This allows the fish to cook slowly and tenderly (it should take approximately 30 minutes). Using a slotted spoon, gently transfer the tuna to kitchen paper to drain.

○ Meanwhile, pre-heat the oven to 200°C/400°F/Gas Mark 6.

○ Place the yellow peppers on a baking tray and roast for 15–20 minutes until tender. Transfer the peppers to a bowl and sprinkle with the garlic, extra virgin olive oil, vinegar, sea salt and freshly ground black pepper.

○ Bring a large pan of salted water to a rolling boil. Add the pasta and return to a rolling boil. Stir the pasta and cook for 3–4 minutes until al dente. Drain, then transfer to a large bowl and mix with the tomatoes, chilli, extra virgin olive oil and basil.

○ Place 2 roasted pepper halves, cut-side up, on 4 large serving plates. Fill the peppers with the angel hair pasta and tuna. Drizzle with extra virgin olive oil and sprinkle with ground black pepper and serve immediately.

Pizza di Patate con Anguille

Potato Pizza with Dandelion and Smoked Eel

This is a pizza I tried in Rome where it was served without eel, but my little extra worked wonders in my bar.

Dandelion leaves are medium length, spiky yellow and quite thick. They have a slightly bitter, grassy taste. They are available in some supermarkets when in season – from late spring. Rocket or any other bitter leaves such as frisée can be use instead – dress with a little balsamic vinegar. For a little extra extravagance, add a few drops of white truffle oil (see page 81) to the potato base while mashing.

SERVES 4
PREPARATION TIME: 30 MINUTES
COOKING TIME: 30 MINUTES

500g (1lb 2oz) floury potatoes, such as King Edwards
55g (2oz) self-raising flour
2 medium eggs, beaten
100ml (3½fl oz) double cream
salt and freshly ground black pepper

FOR THE TOMATO SAUCE

1 x 400g (14oz) can whole plum tomatoes
4 anchovy fillets in oil, drained
5ml (1 teaspoon) chopped fresh oregano leaves
30g (1oz) fresh basil, stalks discarded
75ml (5 tablespoons) extra virgin olive oil

FOR THE TOPPING

3 plum tomatoes, peeled and sliced, juices reserved
4 x 10cm (4in) smoked eel fillets, flaked
225g (8oz) dandelion leaves, washed
juice of 1 lemon

❍ Prick the potatoes with a skewer or fork, place in a large pan, cover with cold water and bring to the boil. Cook for 15–20 minutes until the potatoes are tender. Drain, and when cool enough to handle, peel the potatoes. Return the potatoes to the pan and roughly mash with a potato masher. Mash in the flour, eggs and cream. Season to taste. Set aside.

❍ Meanwhile, place the whole tomatoes and their juices and the anchovies in a pan and boil for 10 minutes until quite pulpy. Stir in the oregano and roughly tear in the basil leaves. Drizzle in a little oil and season to taste, then cook through for 5 minutes.

❍ Place the sliced tomatoes in a dish, drizzle with oil and season to taste.

❍ To make the pizza bases, heat a large frying pan and add a little oil. Quarter the potato mixture and shape into circles in the pan – you can use a large 12cm (5in) pastry cutter in the pan as a guide. Place the potato mixture in the ring and flatten with the back of a metal spoon. Cook for 5 minutes on each side until golden brown.

❍ Top each pizza base with the tomato sauce and sliced tomatoes, then sprinkle over the smoked eel. Put the dandelion leaves in a bowl and drizzle with the lemon juice and remaining olive oil. Season to taste. Curl bunches of the leaves in the palm of your hand, then sit them on the pizzas. Serve immediately.

Maccheroncini al Ragù di Seppie

Baby Macaroni with Cuttlefish Ragù

Ragù is normally associated with meat, but fish is a wonderful alternative, as well as being much quicker to cook. In Italy fish is often used in ragùs and casseroles. Cuttlefish are one of the best fish to use.

SERVES 4
PREPARATION TIME: 20 MINUTES
COOKING TIME: 50 MINUTES

340g (12oz) baby macaroni

FOR THE RAGÙ
120ml (8 tablespoons) olive oil
1 fresh red chilli, halved, seeded and finely chopped
1 garlic clove, unpeeled and bashed
1 garlic clove, finely chopped
450g (1lb) cuttlefish, cleaned and cut into rings
150ml (5fl oz) dry white wine
2 x 400g (14oz) canned peeled plum tomatoes
15g (½oz) fresh basil, stalks discarded
15g (½oz) fresh flat-leaf parsley
15ml (1 tablespoon) salt
5ml (1 teaspoon) freshly ground black pepper

❍ Heat the oil in a frying pan, add the chilli and both garlics and sauté for 1 minute over a medium heat. Add the cuttlefish and the squid and cook for a further 5 minutes. Add the wine and simmer for 2 minutes. Add the tomatoes and cook for 45 minutes. Chop the basil and parsley and add them to the ragù. Season with the salt and black pepper and reduce the heat to low.

❍ Meanwhile, bring a large pan of salted water to a rolling boil. Add the macaroni to the pan and return to a rolling boil. Stir and cook for 5 minutes until al dente. Drain, then add to the ragù. Continue to cook over a low heat for 3 minutes. Serve immediately.

Paglia e Fieno, Funghi e Calamari

Hay and Straw with Shiitake Mushrooms and Squid

The pasta makes this dish very colourful – hence its name – and it also tastes great.
As an alternative to squid, I sometimes use monkfish or octopus, but the cooking will
be a lot longer – 1 hour.
The type of mushrooms used in this recipe is entirely up to you, as long as they have lots
of flavour. Shiitake are now widely available in supermarkets, but you can try porcini for
special occasions when in season; another good type to try are girolles.

SERVES 4
PREPARATION TIME: 45 MINUTES
COOKING TIME: 10 MINUTES

1 quantity Basic White Pasta Dough (see page 172)
1 quantity Basic Spinach Pasta Dough
(see page 173)

FOR THE SAUCE
60ml (4 tablespoons) extra virgin olive oil
340g (12oz) baby squid, cleaned (see page 12) and
sliced into thin strips

2 fat garlic cloves, crushed
170g (6oz) shiitake mushrooms, wiped, trimmed
and sliced
150ml (5fl oz) dry white wine
170g (6oz) peeled prawns, patted dry with kitchen
paper
45ml (3 tablespoons) chopped fresh flat-leaf parsley
170g (6oz) unsalted butter, diced and chilled
salt and freshly ground black pepper

❍ Use a pasta machine to roll out the pasta and cut into fettuccine. Lay the pasta out on 1–2 large trays, cover with cling film and set aside.

❍ Bring a large pan of salted water to a rolling boil.

❍ Heat half of the oil in a heavy-based pan. Add the baby squid and cook gently for 1 minute. Stir in the garlic and mushrooms and cook for 2 minutes, then add the wine. Bring to the boil and cook for 1 minute. Stir in the prawns and parsley. Gradually stir in the butter until the texture is velvety smooth.

❍ Add the pasta to the pan of boiling water and return to a rolling boil. Stir and cook for 4 minutes until al dente. Drain, reserving 150ml (5fl oz) of the cooking liquid.

❍ Add the pasta to the squid and mushroom sauce and toss to mix. Add some of the reserved cooking liquid if the mixture is too dry. Season to taste. Divide the pasta among large pasta bowls and drizzle with the remaining oil. Serve immediately.

Penne al Branzino e Pomodoro

Penne with Sea Bass and Tomato

You may think that sea bass is quite extravagant to serve with penne, but you will not regret it. Something that the Italians love to do is to finish off recipes with a drizzling of good quality extra virgin olive oil – it acts as a brilliantly simple 'sauce'.

SERVES 4
PREPARATION TIME: 25 MINUTES
COOKING TIME: 25 MINUTES

675g (1½lb) sea bass fillets
55g (2oz) butter
1 celery stick, trimmed and finely diced
1 medium onion, finely chopped
2 garlic cloves, finely diced

1 bulb fennel, trimmed and finely diced
15ml (1 tablespoon) fennel seeds
4 beef tomatoes, peeled, seeded and diced
(see page 26)
340g (12oz) penne
30ml (2 tablespoons) olive oil
salt and freshly ground black pepper
extra virgin olive oil, to drizzle

❍ Using a pair of tweezers, remove any bones from the sea bass (see page 10). Cut the fillets into 4 or 8 pieces. Set aside.

❍ Bring a large pan of salted water to a rolling boil.

❍ Melt the butter in a large pan, add the celery, onion, garlic and diced fennel and cook gently for 10 minutes until soft. Stir in the fennel seeds and cook for 1 minute. Stir in the tomatoes, season to taste and simmer for 10 minutes.

❍ Meanwhile, add the pasta to the pan of boiling water and return to a rolling boil. Stir and cook for

10–12 minutes until al dente. Drain, reserving 150ml (5fl oz) the cooking liquid.

❍ Heat the olive oil in a large heavy-based frying pan and add the fish, flesh-side down. Cook for 2 minutes, then turn the fish over and cook for a further 2 minutes. Season to taste.

❍ Stir the cooked penne into the fennel sauce. Add some of the reserved cooking liquid if the pasta is a little dry. Spoon the penne onto a large warmed platter and place the sea bass on top. Drizzle with extra virgin olive oil and serve immediately.

Tagliolini alla Crema di Zafferano e Cozze

Home-made Tagliolini with Saffron and Mussel Sauce

This is a perfect marriage between sauce and pasta because this very thin, flat spaghetti absorbs creamy sauces beautifully. Serve with a chilled glass or two of Pinot Grigio.

SERVES 4
PREPARATION TIME: 45 MINUTES
COOKING TIME: 10 MINUTES

340g (12oz) tagliolini (see page 172 for the Basic White Pasta Dough)
60ml (4 tablespoons) extra virgin olive oil
2 garlic cloves, crushed

2 good pinches of saffron strands
500g (1lb 2oz) mussels, scrubbed clean, beards and barnacles removed
150ml (5fl oz) dry white wine
300ml (10fl oz) double cream
30g (1oz) flat-leaf parsley, tough stalks discarded and roughly chopped
salt and freshly ground black pepper

❍ Use a pasta machine to roll out and cut the pasta dough into thin tagliolini strands. Place on a tray, cover with cling film and set aside.

❍ Bring a large pan of salted water to a rolling boil.

❍ Meanwhile, heat the oil in a deep heavy-based pan, add the garlic and cook for 1 minute. Place the saffron and mussels in the pan, cover tightly and cook over a high heat for 3–5 minutes, shaking the pan frequently, until the shells have opened. Add the wine to the pan, cover and cook over a low heat for 3 minutes. Discard any mussels that have remained closed. Add the cream, heat gently and season to taste.

❍ Meanwhile, add the pasta to the pan of boiling water and return to a rolling boil. Stir and cook for 3 minutes until al dente. Drain, reserving 150ml (5fl oz) of the cooking liquid. Add the pasta and parsley to the mussels and stir to mix. Add some of the reserved cooking liquid if the mixture is a little dry. Cook for 30 seconds. Serve immediately.

Spaghetti all'Astice e Carciofi

Spaghetti with Artichokes and Lobster

While many people regard spaghetti as everyday fare, here it is lifted to luxury level with the addition of lobster and artichokes. The flavour is heavenly, and if you're planning a special dinner party, this is a dish that you should keep in mind for serving.

SERVES 4
PREPARATION TIME: 30 MINUTES
COOKING TIME: 20 MINUTES

4 young fresh artichokes
juice of 1 lemon
4 plum tomatoes, peeled, seeded and chopped (see page 26)
12 fresh basil leaves, torn
60ml (4 tablespoons) chopped fresh flat-leaf parsley

3 garlic cloves, chopped
60ml (4 tablespoons) extra virgin olive oil
4 shallots, finely chopped
2 x 450g (1lb) lobsters, cooked (see page 11), shelled and the meat cut into large chunks
60ml (2fl oz) brandy
150ml (5fl oz) dry white wine
170g (6oz) spaghetti
salt and freshly ground black pepper

❍ Bring 2 large pans of salted water to a rolling boil.

❍ Meanwhile, quarter the artichokes and scoop out the hairy chokes with a teaspoon. Rub the lemon juice all over to prevent discolouring. Add the artichokes to one pan of boiling water and cook for 3–4 minutes until tender. Drain.

❍ Mix together the tomatoes, basil, parsley and half of the garlic.

❍ Heat half of the oil in a large heavy-based frying pan, add the shallots and the remaining garlic and cook for 3–4 minutes until soft. Stir in the lobster. Pour over the brandy and ignite. Once the flames die down, add the tomato mixture and the wine. Simmer for 5–8 minutes until the juices reduce slightly. Season to taste.

❍ Meanwhile, ease the spaghetti into the second pan of boiling water and return to a rolling boil. Stir and cook for 5–8 minutes until al dente. Drain. Add the pasta and artichokes to the sauce, tossing well to mix. Adjust the seasoning, if necessary. Divide the pasta among large warmed serving plates and drizzle with the remaining oil. Serve immediately.

Gnocchi al Pesce

Shellfish Gnocchi

Gnocchi are small potato dumplings and in Italy we always eat them as a first course. They are not usually served with fish but I put this dish on one of my menus recently and it was a great success. If you have the time, I would suggest making your own gnocchi – the final result will be much better than using bought gnocchi.

SERVES 4
PREPARATION TIME: 30 MINUTES
COOKING TIME: 45 MINUTES

340g (12oz) gnocchi (see page 174)
salt and freshly ground black pepper

FOR THE SEMI-DRIED TOMATOES
5 plum tomatoes, quartered
5ml (1 teaspoon) sea salt
15ml (1 tablespoon) balsamic vinegar
30ml (2 tablespoons) extra virgin olive oil

FOR THE SAUCE
30ml (2 tablespoons) extra virgin olive oil
1 carrot, finely diced
1 celery stalk, trimmed and diced
1 onion, finely diced
1 garlic clove, crushed
2 bay leaves
2 sprigs of fresh thyme, leaves chopped
1 sprig of fresh rosemary, leaves chopped
150ml (5fl oz) dry white wine
250g (9oz) clams, washed clean
500g (1lb 2oz) mussels, scrubbed clean, beards and barnacles removed

❍ Pre-heat the oven to 190°C/375°F/Gas Mark 5. Line a roasting tin with foil and place the tomatoes, skin-side down, on top. Sprinkle with the sea salt, 15ml (1 tablespoon) black pepper, vinegar and oil. Roast for 30 minutes until all the liquid has evaporated and the tomatoes are slightly charred.

❍ Heat the oil in a large pan and add the carrot, celery, onion, garlic and herbs. Stir well, then cook for 8 minutes until just beginning to soften but not brown. Add the wine and cook for 5–7 minutes.

❍ Meanwhile, place the mussels and clams with 90ml (6 tablespoons) water in a large deep pan. Cover with a tight-fitting lid and cook over high heat for 3–5 minutes, shaking the pan frequently, until the shells are completely open.

❍ Strain the pan juices through a fine sieve and return them to the pan. Boil the juices for 2 minutes to reduce by half. Remove half of the shells from the mussels and clams. Discard any shellfish that have remained closed.

❍ Bring a large pan of salted water to the boil. Add the gnocchi, then stir and cook for 3–5 minutes until they rise to the surface and are al dente. Drain.

❍ Add the gnocchi, shellfish and tomatoes to the vegetable mixture and toss to mix. Stir in the pan juices and season well to taste. Discard the bay leaves and serve immediately.

Pizza al Salmone e Spinaci

Smoked Salmon and Spinach Pizza

I think it's a great idea to introduce children to fish at a young age. They love pizza and this way they'll be eating their greens, too.

SERVES 4
PREPARATION TIME: 30 MINUTES PLUS
15 MINUTES RESTING
COOKING TIME: 20 MINUTES

FOR THE PIZZA BASE
500g (1lb 2oz) 00 flour
15ml (1 tablespoon) salt
1 x 15g (½oz) sachet easy-blend yeast
75ml (5 tablespoons) extra virgin olive oil
150ml (5fl oz) warm water

FOR THE TOPPING
45ml (3 tablespoons) extra virgin olive oil
1 red onion, sliced
100g (3½oz) packet prepared baby spinach, finely
shredded
60ml (4 tablespoons) soured cream
grated zest and juice of 1 lemon
4 slices smoked salmon, cut into very thin slices
salt and freshly ground black pepper
lemon wedges, to serve

❍ Sift the flour and salt into a large bowl and stir in the yeast. Add the oil and rub it into the flour to make rough breadcrumbs. Stir in the water to form a dough. Knead on a lightly floured surface for 5 minutes until quite elastic. Cover with cling film and allow to rest for 15 minutes.

❍ Meanwhile, heat half of the oil in a large frying pan, add the onion and cook for 5 minutes until soft. Stir in the spinach and cook for 1 minute. Remove the pan from the heat and season to taste.

❍ Pre-heat the oven to 225°C/425°F/Gas Mark 7.

❍ You may need to work in batches: roll out the pizza dough into four 15–20cm (6in–8in) thin circles and transfer to baking trays. Spread each pizza base with half of the soured cream and sprinkle with the lemon zest and juice. Top with the spinach and onion mixture, then ruffles of the smoked salmon. Drizzle with the remaining oil and plenty of black pepper. Bake for 10–15 minutes until the base is crisp and golden. Serve immediately with lemon wedges.

Fusilli al Tonno

Fusilli with Tuna

My daughter Laura loves tuna, particularly the canned variety! When she first visited Zilli Fish, she ordered tuna pasta, thinking it would be canned, but she was very pleased with the fresh tuna that was served. You can use either, depending on your preference.

SERVES 4
PREPARATION TIME: 15 MINUTES
COOKING TIME: 15 MINUTES

340g (12oz) fusilli or pasta twists
60ml (4 tablespoons) extra virgin olive oil
2 garlic cloves, crushed
2 medium courgettes, trimmed and diced
340g (12oz) fresh tuna, diced

150ml (5fl oz) dry white wine
900g (2lb) ripe plum tomatoes, peeled, seeded and diced (see page 26)
125g (4½oz) capers, drained and patted dry with kitchen paper
60ml (4 tablespoons) chopped fresh flat-leaf parsley
15g (½oz) fresh basil, stalks discarded and leaves torn
salt and freshly ground black pepper

❍ Bring a large pan of salted water to a rolling boil. Add the pasta to the pan and return to a rolling boil. Stir and cook for 10 minutes until al dente.

❍ Meanwhile, heat the oil in a large heavy-based frying pan. Add the garlic and courgettes and cook for 3–4 minutes. Stir in the tuna and cook for 1 minute. Add the wine and allow to bubble for 2 minutes. Add the tomatoes, capers, parsley and basil. Season to taste.

❍ Drain the pasta, reserving 150ml (5fl oz) of the cooking liquid. Add the pasta to the tuna sauce and toss to mix. Add some of the reserved cooking liquid to moisten the mixture. Cook for 30 seconds to heat through. Adjust the seasoning, if necessary. Sprinkle with extra black pepper and serve immediately.

Main Courses

Tonno ai Peperoni

Chargrilled Tuna with Red Peppers

To chargrill food at home either means using a barbecue (impossible in the winter), or cooking the food on a hob-top grill pan – fast-becoming a popular option. Called a ridged grill pan, it is made of cast-iron and has ridges which characteristically score the food. The grill pan is quite inexpensive, and the more you use it the better its non-sticking qualities become. Chargrilling is a very healthy and tasty method of cooking – very little, if any, oil is required and the food is sealed quickly, enclosing all the succulent juices of fish, meat and vegetables.

Deep-fried herbs add a delicious touch to dishes. Wash and dry the leaves and deep-fry in small batches for 30 seconds. Remove and drain on kitchen paper.

SERVES 4
PREPARATION TIME: 30 MINUTES PLUS
1 HOUR MARINATING
COOKING TIME: 4 MINUTES

3 large red peppers, charred, skinned and seeded
(see page 171)
1 garlic clove, crushed

60ml (4 tablespoons) extra virgin olive oil
60ml (4 tablespoons) vintage balsamic vinegar
30ml (2 tablespoons) chopped fresh flat-leaf parsley
4 x 170g (6oz) tuna fillets
salt and freshly ground black pepper
12 large fresh basil leaves, deep-fried, to garnish
(optional)

❍ Slice the red peppers into long thin strips, place in a bowl, add the garlic, 45ml (3 tablespoons) of the oil, vinegar and parsley. Season to taste. Mix well and allow to marinate for 1 hour.

❍ Drizzle the remaining oil over the tuna and season to taste.

❍ Pre-heat a ridged cast-iron grill pan until smoking. Place the tuna on the grill pan and cook for 2 minutes on each side – the tuna should still be rare in the centre.

❍ Allow the tuna to rest for 2 minutes, then thinly slice. Spoon half of the red pepper sauce into the centre of 4 serving plates, then top with the sliced tuna. Top each with some of the remaining sauce and drizzle over the remaining juices. Garnish with basil leaves, if desired, and serve immediately.

Salmone Cremonese

Salmon with Samphire and Mostarda di Cremona

As the name implies, the fruits used in the Italian preserve *Mostarda di Cremona*, which include pears, figs, apricots and cherries in mustard and honey, come from Cremona. The preserve is available from Italian delis. It would also go well with the Mosaic of Mixed Fish (see page 133).

For a special occasion use wild salmon if available, otherwise farmed salmon is good. Ideally use fillets that have been cut from the middle of the fish as this will allow the fish to cook evenly.

Samphire, also referred to as 'sea asparagus', is often thought of as a type of seaweed but actually it is a sea vegetable. It has a short season in the summer, so make the most of it and use as a garnish or accompaniment for all seafood. It needs to be rinsed well before using and cooked simply – just blanch it in boiling water for a few minutes, and do not add salt when cooking as samphire does tend to be quite salty.

SERVES 4
PREPARATION TIME: 15 MINUTES
COOKING TIME: 8–10 MINUTES

60ml (4 tablespoons) olive oil
4 x 170g (6oz) wild salmon fillets, scaled and pin-boned (see page 10)

225g (8oz) samphire, washed and patted dry with kitchen paper
45ml (3 tablespoons) extra virgin olive oil
15ml (1 tablespoon) fresh lemon juice
1 small jar *Mostarda di Cremona*, drained and roughly chopped
salt and freshly ground black pepper

○ Heat 30ml (2 tablespoons) of the olive oil in a large non-stick pan.

○ Season the salmon fillets, skin-side up, to taste. Place in the hot oil, skin-side down. Cook for about 5 minutes. The skin should be brown and crisp. Turn the fillets over and cook for a further 2 minutes, then transfer to a plate and keep warm.

○ Add the remaining olive oil to the same pan, then add the samphire. Sauté over a high heat for 1 minute (do not season), then spoon it into the centre of 4 serving plates. Place the salmon fillets, skin-side up, on the samphire. Mix the extra virgin olive oil with the lemon juice and drizzle over the fish, then spoon the *Mostarda di Cremona* around the fish. Serve immediately.

Fritto Misto

Deep-Fried Fish with Anchovy Mayonnaise

Fritto misto is one of those classic Italian specialities that just doesn't date. Use the freshest ingredients – the mixture of fish and shellfish is entirely up to you. Salmon works extremely well as do cod, partly shelled langoustines and squid rings and tentacles. Keep the fish thin and finger-sized so they cook quickly. To be enjoyed at their best, you need to serve the fritto misto as soon as they are cooked.

This has always been a popular dish in my restaurants over the years. When I put it on the Zilli Fish menu last year it swam out of the kitchen!

SERVES 4
PREPARATION TIME: 30 MINUTES
COOKING TIME: 15 MINUTES

FOR THE BATTER
340g (12oz) self-raising flour
750ml (1¼ pints) cold water
salt and freshly ground black pepper

FOR THE SEAFOOD
4 king scallops, washed, patted dry and halved if thick
125g (4½oz) squid, cleaned (see page 12) and cut into rings
125g (4½oz) salmon fillet, skinned, pin-boned (see page 10) and cut into fingers

4 langoustines, if live plunge into boiling water for 30 seconds, drain and cool
125g (4½oz) cod fillet, skinned, pin-boned (see page 10) and cut into fingers
125g (4½oz) swordfish fillet, skinned and cut into fingers
125g (4oz) halibut fillet, skinned and cut into fingers
90ml (6 tablespoons) plain flour
vegetable oil for deep-frying
lemon wedges, to serve

FOR THE ANCHOVY MAYONNAISE
300ml (10fl oz) Mayonnaise (see page 166)
6 salted anchovy fillets, soaked in milk for 5 minutes, drained and finely chopped
30ml (2 tablespoons) finely chopped fresh parsley

❍ Put the self-raising flour into a large bowl and season well. Gradually whisk in the water to form a smooth batter. Cover and set aside for 10 minutes.

❍ Meanwhile, pat the fish dry with kitchen paper, keeping the different types of seafood separate, and season well. Spread the flour on a large plate.

❍ Pour enough oil for deep-frying into a deep frying pan over a medium heat. Heat until a piece of bread dropped in the oil sizzles and turns golden brown in 30 seconds.

❍ Working in batches, coat the seafood in the plain flour, shake off the surplus, then dip it into the batter and deep-fry for 1–2 minutes until crisp. Using a slotted spoon, drain the fish well, then transfer to kitchen paper to drain again. Keep warm until all the seafood is fried.

❍ Mix all the ingredients together for the anchovy mayonnaise and spoon into 1 large or 4 separate dipping bowls. Arrange the fritto misto in a large bowl or platter and serve immediately with the mayonnaise and lemon wedges.

Filetti di Passera in Salsa di Vongole

Fillet of Plaice with Clam Sauce

Plaice is a great British favourite. It's a very delicate fish and therefore it needs to be cooked as simply and as quickly as possible. Serve it with a good flavoursome sauce that can be spooned over it – the minute you try to stir it the fish will just break up. Serve this dish with small new potatoes cooked in their skins.

SERVES 4
PREPARATION TIME: 20 MINUTES PLUS
30 MINUTES SOAKING
COOKING TIME: 10 MINUTES

450g (1lb) live *palourde* (Venus) clams
30ml (2 tablespoons) extra virgin olive oil

175ml (6fl oz) dry white wine
240ml (8fl oz) Fish Stock (see page 164)
170g (6oz) unsalted butter, diced and chilled
60ml (4 tablespoons) chopped fresh flat-leaf parsley
4 fresh basil leaves, torn
4 x 170g (6oz) plaice fillets, skinned and trimmed
salt and freshly ground black pepper

❍ Soak the clams in salted water for 30 minutes to remove the grit, then wash in clean water, scrub clean and drain.

❍ Heat half of the oil in a heavy-based deep pan, then add the clams, cover tightly and cook over a high heat for 3 minutes, shaking the pan gently, until the clams just start to open. Add the wine and stock, cover the pan again and cook the clams for a further 2 minutes. Discard any clams that have remained closed.

❍ Add the butter to the pan and stir continuously over a high heat until blended into the juices. Strain the sauce through a sieve and return to the pan. Add half of the parsley and all of the basil leaves and season to taste. Remove from heat and set aside.

❍ Pre-heat the grill to hot.

❍ Season the plaice fillets, brush with the remaining oil and place under the grill. Cook for 3–4 minutes on one side only until lightly cooked. Carefully transfer the plaice to 4 warmed serving plates and spoon over the clams and the sauce. Sprinkle with the remaining parsley and serve immediately.

Rösti di Salmone e Patate

Salmon *Rösti*

Salmon lends itself to many different types of cooking methods, but this one works wonderfully and the result tastes as good as it looks. If you like, instead of flipping over the salmon and potato, you can turn it over like a tortilla; just invert the salmon on to a large plate, then slip it back into the pan with the *rösti* on the bottom.

SERVES 4
PREPARATION TIME: 30 MINUTES
COOKING TIME: 20 MINUTES

340g (12oz) waxy potatoes, peeled and coarsely grated
2 medium egg yolks, lightly beaten
4 x 170g (6oz) salmon fillets, skinned and pin-boned (see page 10)
15ml (1 tablespoon) plain flour
75ml (5 tablespoons) olive oil
55g (2oz) unsalted butter
sunflower oil for deep-frying

FOR THE SAUCE
55g (2oz) unsalted butter
1 medium leek, trimmed and finely chopped
15g (½oz) fresh chives, reserving 8 whole chives for the garnish and chopping the remainder
300ml (10fl oz) double cream
salt and freshly ground black pepper

❍ Pour enough oil for deep-frying into a deep frying pan over a medium heat. Heat until a piece of bread dropped in the oil sizzles and turns golden brown in 30 seconds.

❍ Working in batches, plunge the grated potatoes into the hot oil and blanch for 30 seconds. Using a slotted spoon, drain the potatoes well then transfer to kitchen paper to drain again. Allow to cool.

❍ Meanwhile, melt the butter in a small pan, and add the leeks and chives. Cover with a damp piece of greaseproof paper (the paper should touch the vegetables), then a tight-fitting lid. Cook (sweat) the vegetables over a low heat for 5–8 minutes until soft. Remove the greaseproof paper and stir in the cream. Bring to a simmer and cook for 2 minutes. Pour the sauce into a blender and process until smooth. Return the sauce to the pan and season to taste. Set aside.

❍ Put the cooled potatoes in a bowl, season to taste and mix with the egg yolks. Season the salmon fillets, dust with the flour and press the potato mixture on to one side of each salmon fillet.

❍ Heat the oil in a heavy-based frying pan, then add the butter. When the butter is foaming, add the salmon fillets, potato-side down. Cook for 5 minutes until crisp and golden brown, then quickly flip over the fillets and cook for a further 3 minutes.

❍ Transfer the salmon to 4 warmed serving plates and surround with the sauce. Garnish each with a criss-cross of the reserved chives. Serve immediately.

Paillard di Pesce Spada, Rucola e Peperoni

Swordfish Steaks on Rocket and Roast Peppers

This very simple dish is perfect for a summer lunch, but it also looks impressive as a main course for a dinner party. Serve it with angel hair pasta in a butter and lemon sauce.

SERVES 4
PREPARATION TIME: 30 MINUTES PLUS
1 HOUR MARINATING
COOKING TIME: 15 MINUTES

90ml (6 tablespoons) extra virgin olive oil
finely grated zest of 1 lemon
finely grated zest of 1 small orange
15ml (1 tablespoon) chopped fresh oregano
8 x 75g (3oz) swordfish steaks
salt and freshly ground black pepper

FOR THE YELLOW PEPPER SALSA
1 red pepper
1 yellow pepper

60ml (4 tablespoons) extra virgin olive oil
juice of ½ lemon
juice of ½ orange
8–10 fresh basil leaves, torn
15ml (1 tablespoon) roughly chopped fresh
flat-leaf parsley
1 bunch spring onions, trimmed and
sliced diagonally

FOR THE SALAD
125g (4½oz) rocket
125g (4½oz) radicchio
30ml (2 tablespoons) extra virgin olive oil
15ml (1 tablespoon) lemon juice

❍ In a large shallow dish, mix together the oil, lemon and orange zests, oregano and plenty of black pepper. Place the swordfish in the marinade, then turn to coat all over. Cover with cling film and leave at room temperature to marinate for 1 hour.

❍ Pre-heat a ridged cast-iron grill pan until hot.

❍ Place the peppers on the grill pan and cook for 5–8 minutes, turning frequently until the peppers are just soft and slightly charred in several places. Cool the peppers slightly, then halve and seed; do not peel. Cut the peppers into small diamond shapes and mix with the oil, lemon and orange juices, basil, parsley and spring onions. Season to taste. Cover with cling film and set aside.

❍ Wipe the grill pan clean and reheat until it is almost smoking.

❍ Lift the fish out of the marinade and shake to remove any excess oil. Place on the heated grill pan and cook for 1 minute, then turn the fish 45 degrees and cook for 1 minute. Turn the fish over and repeat. You should have criss-cross lines on both sides of the fish.

❍ Wash and spin dry the salad leaves. Put them in a bowl, toss with the oil and lemon juice and season to taste. Put a fish fillet on to each serving plate and spoon a little salsa over it. Top with the salad and then the remaining fish fillet. Spoon the remaining salsa over the fish salad and serve immediately.

Scampi al Curry

Scampi in a Light Curry Sauce

Fresh scampi in Italy are the equivalent of langoustines in this country. To make life easier use frozen scampi for this recipe – they're also more widely available. Serve with cooked fragrant rice.

SERVES 4
PREPARATION TIME: 20 MINUTES
COOKING TIME: 25 MINUTES

900g (2lb) frozen jumbo scampi, thawed
75ml (5 tablespoons) plain flour
15ml (1 tablespoon) crushed sea salt
30ml (2 tablespoons) vegetable oil

FOR THE CURRY SAUCE
45g (1½oz) butter
2 garlic cloves, crushed
4 spring onions, trimmed and finely chopped
45ml (3 tablespoons) madras curry powder
2.5ml (½ teaspoon) ground ginger
300ml (10fl oz) Fish Stock (see page 164)
30g (1oz) coconut cream
45ml (3 tablespoons) roughly chopped fresh coriander
freshly ground black pepper

❍ Pat the scampi dry with kitchen paper. Put 60ml (4 tablespoons) of flour and the sea salt in a bowl, add the scampi and toss to coat.

❍ Heat the oil in a large non-stick pan until hot. Working in batches, add the scampi and cook for 2 minutes on each side. Using a slotted spoon, drain the fish well, then transfer to kitchen paper to drain.

❍ Melt 30g (1oz) butter in the pan and, when foaming, sauté the garlic and spring onions for 2 minutes until golden brown. Stir in curry powder and ginger and cook for 1 minute. Add the stock and coconut cream and simmer for 5 minutes.

❍ Mix together the remaining butter and flour. Gradually whisk the mixture into the sauce and continue cooking until slightly thickened. Add the scampi and cook for a further 3 minutes. Season to taste. Sprinkle with coriander and serve immediately.

Dentice in Guazzetto di Cozze e Patate

Snapper in Mussel and Potato Broth

Snapper is quite a bony fish. To feed two people you'll need an 800g–1kg (1¾–2¼lb) fish. Here, however, I've used snapper fillets. By adding mussels and potatoes you get a good filling meal!

SERVES 4
PREPARATION TIME: 30 MINUTES
COOKING TIME: 30 MINUTES

450g (1lb) new potatoes, peeled
15ml (1 tablespoon) vinegar
30ml (2 tablespoons) crushed sea salt
500g (1lb 2oz) mussels, scrubbed clean, beards and barnacles removed

2 x 340g (12oz) snapper fillets, halved through the middle
150ml (5fl oz) Fish Stock (see page 164)
30ml (2 tablespoons) extra virgin olive oil
15g (½oz) fresh mint, stalks discarded and leaves roughly chopped
2 large sprigs of fresh rosemary, stalks discarded and leaves roughly chopped
salt and freshly ground black pepper

❍ Put the potatoes in a large heavy-based pan and cover with water. Add the vinegar and sea salt and bring to the boil. Cook for 20 minutes until soft. Drain, reserving the cooking liquid.

❍ Return half of the cooking liquid to the pan (reserve the remainder) and add the mussels. Cover tightly and cook over a high heat for 3–5 minutes, shaking the pan frequently, until the shells have opened.

❍ Meanwhile, pour the reserved potato cooking liquid into a large frying pan and add the snapper fillets. Simmer gently for 5 minutes until the fish is just tender when pierced.

❍ Drain the mussels and discard any that have remained closed. Remove and discard the shells from the mussels, then add the mussels to the snapper. Pour in the stock and oil and sprinkle with the mint and rosemary. Gently add the potatoes to the pan. Simmer for 3 minutes and season to taste.

❍ Divide the potatoes, mussels and snapper among 4 large bowls and ladle in the broth. Serve immediately.

Merluzzo, Ceci e Zucchine

Cod with Chick Pea and Courgette Stew

Cod is probably the most popular fish in this country and the most readily available. My mother always used salt cod and soaked it for days but life is too hectic for that now, so here is a modern alternative. This recipe is healthy, good value and very easy to make too. I also like to make this recipe with *cavolo nero* (black cabbage) when in season, and spinach.

SERVES 4
PREPARATION TIME: 20 MINUTES
COOKING TIME: 30 MINUTES

90ml (6 tablespoons) extra virgin olive oil
5ml (1 teaspoon) chopped fresh rosemary leaves
1 bay leaf
1 large onion, finely diced
1 stick celery, trimmed and chopped
1 medium carrot, chopped
1 small fresh red chilli, seeded and chopped

900g (2lb) courgettes, trimmed and chopped
4 sun-dried tomatoes, finely diced
2 x 400g (14oz) can chick peas, drained and washed
150ml (5fl oz) Fish Stock (see page 164)
30ml (2 tablespoons) chopped fresh flat-leaf parsley
juice of ½ lemon
45ml (3 tablespoons) plain flour
2 fat garlic cloves, sliced
4 x 170g (6oz) cod fillets, pin-boned (see page 10)
salt and freshly ground black pepper

❍ Heat one-third of oil in a deep pan until hot. Add the rosemary and bay leaf and cook for 1 minute. Stir in the onion, celery, carrot and chilli and cook for 7–8 minutes until soft. Add the courgettes and sun-dried tomatoes and cook for a further 3–5 minutes until the courgettes are al dente. Add the chick peas and stock and simmer for 10 minutes. Add the parsley, lemon juice and seasoning and simmer for 5 minutes.

❍ Meanwhile, spread the flour on a flat plate and season with salt and pepper. Heat the remaining oil

in a frying pan, add the garlic and fry for 3 minutes, then remove and discard them. Coat the fish in the seasoned flour and add them to the pan, skin-side down. Cook for 5 minutes until golden brown, then flip the fish over and cook for a further 3 minutes. The fish should just flake.

❍ Divide the stew among 4 warmed deep plates and place the fish on top. Serve immediately.

Sogliola di Dover al Burro e Limone

Dover Sole with Lemon Butter and Parsley

I believe this is one of the best ways of cooking Dover sole, a delicately flavoured but firm-fleshed fish. We are lucky in the UK to be able to get sole which is so fresh and big.

SERVES 4
PREPARATION TIME: 15 MINUTES
COOKING TIME: 10 MINUTES

4 x 340g (12oz) Dover sole, cleaned
30ml (2 tablespoons) plain flour
60ml (4 tablespoons) sunflower oil

125g (4½oz) butter
juice of 2 lemons
1 lemon, sliced into rounds
30g (1oz) fresh flat-leaf parsley, stalks discarded
and leaves roughly chopped
30ml (2 tablespoons) sea salt
15ml (1 tablespoon) freshly ground black pepper

❍ Pat the fish dry with kitchen paper, then dust with the flour.

❍ Put the oil in a large non-stick frying pan and heat until hot. Add 30g (1oz) of the butter and heat until foaming.

❍ Pre-heat the grill to medium.

❍ Place the Dover sole in the frying pan and cook for 3 minutes on each side, then place the pan under the grill and cook the fish for a further 3 minutes.

To check if the fish is cooked, open it slightly in the middle, and if the bone is clear of any blood the fish is ready.

❍ Melt the remaining butter in a separate frying pan. Add the lemon juice and slices and cook for 2–3 minutes. Stir in the parsley and cook for 1 minute.

❍ Transfer the fish to 4 large serving plates and pour the sauce over it. Sprinkle with sea salt and black pepper and serve immediately.

Orata Abbottonata

Bream with Garlic and Rosemary

The Italian version of this fish dish is extremely popular in my village. I first cooked it in a wood-burning oven, and as all of these flavours stayed with me you'll often find it on my menu when it's available (but not cooked in the wood-burning oven). It's lovely with roasted fennel and a glass of chilled Pinot Grigio del Trentino, but you can also serve it simply with a mixed salad.

SERVES 4
PREPARATION TIME: 15 MINUTES
COOKING TIME: 20 MINUTES

4 garlic cloves, chopped
30ml (2 tablespoons) dried breadcrumbs
3 large sprigs of fresh rosemary, tough stalks discarded and leaves chopped
2.5ml (½ teaspoon) English mustard powder
4 x 450g (1lb) whole breams, scaled and cleaned
45ml (3 tablespoons) plain flour
90ml (3fl oz) vegetable oil
15g (½oz) butter
30ml (2 tablespoons) olive oil
salt and freshly ground black pepper

◯ Pre-heat the oven to 200°C/400°F/Gas Mark 6.

◯ Mix together the garlic, breadcrumbs, rosemary and mustard powder.

◯ Pat the fish dry with kitchen paper, then open them out and put 15ml (1 tablespoon) of the herb mixture inside each one. Cut 3 slashes on both sides of each fish. Spread the flour on a flat plate and season with salt and pepper. Coat the fish in the seasoned flour.

◯ Heat the vegetable oil in a large non-stick ovenproof frying pan. When hot, add the butter and cook until foaming. Place the fish in the pan and cook for 3–4 minutes on each side until golden brown. Sprinkle over the remaining herb mixture and drizzle with the olive oil.

◯ Place the frying pan in the oven and bake the fish for 10 minutes. To check if it's cooked, take a sharp knife and place it in the middle of the fish; if it comes out hot then the fish is ready to serve.

Portafoglio di Pescatrice con Pancetta Affumicata

Monkfish Parcels with Smoked Pancetta

Monkfish is a firm fish, but it can be quite bland if it is served plain. It can take good strong flavours, as here where the fish is wrapped in smoked pancetta or bacon. Serve the monkfish on a platter of squid ink pasta; stunning for a dinner party.

SERVES 4–6
PREPARATION TIME: 30 MINUTES
COOKING TIME: 25 MINUTES

½ small red pepper
½ small green pepper
½ small yellow pepper
2 x 340g (12oz) monkfish fillets, trimmed and membrane removed
125g (4½oz) smoked pancetta, thinly sliced
1 large sprig of fresh rosemary, separated into sprigs
60ml (4 tablespoons) extra virgin olive oil

FOR THE PASTA
1 quantity shop-bought squid ink pasta
60ml (4 tablespoons) extra virgin olive oil
1 plump garlic clove, crushed
1 medium courgette, halved lengthways, seeded and thinly sliced
4 plum tomatoes, peeled, seeded and diced (see page 26)
30ml (2 tablespoons) chopped fresh flat-leaf parsley
salt and freshly ground black pepper

❍ Pre-heat the oven to 200°C/400°F/Gas Mark 6.

❍ Cut away the membranes from the red, yellow and green peppers, then slice the peppers very finely into strips. Season the monkfish all over.

❍ Lay the pancetta out flat with each slice slightly overlapping, then arrange half of the peppers along the centre. Place the monkfish on top, and arrange the remaining pepper slices and half of the rosemary on the fish. Tightly roll the ends of the pancetta around the monkfish, then pierce the pancetta with the remaining rosemary sprigs.

❍ Heat a large heavy-based ovenproof frying pan until hot, add the 60ml (4 tablespoons) of oil and heat until hot. Add the monkfish and seal for

5 minutes, turning the fish constantly. Transfer the pan to the oven and roast for 10 minutes, then turn off the oven and open the door slightly – this will keep the fish warm while the pasta is cooking.

❍ Bring a large pan of salted water to a rolling boil. Add the squid ink pasta to the pan of boiling water and return to a rolling boil. Stir the pasta and cook for 3–4 minutes until al dente. Drain.

❍ Meanwhile, heat the oil in a large frying pan. Add the garlic and courgettes and cook for 3 minutes until slightly soft. Stir in the tomatoes and parsley. Add the pasta, season to taste and stir until the pasta is coated.

❍ Spoon the pasta on to a platter and place the wrapped monkfish on top. Serve immediately.

Astice al Burro e Aglio con Patatine

Grilled Lobster, Garlic Butter and Chips

This is a magnificently glorified fish and chips! A great treat and yet still extremely simple to prepare, it remains one of the best sellers in Zilli Fish. Try it with a glass of Gavi di Gavi. The best varieties of potatoes to use for chips are King Edwards, Desirée, Romano or Maris Piper. The potatoes need to be washed and soaked in cold water for 10 minutes to remove some of the starch before frying. Then fry in a good quality groundnut oil as it can be heated to a much higher temperature than most of the other oils. The potatoes need to be fried twice for that perfect crispness. You'll also find that frying chips in an oil that has been used a couple of times before gives a much better golden colour.

SERVES 4
PREPARATION TIME: 25 MINUTES
COOKING TIME: 15 MINUTES

900g (2lb) potatoes for chips, peeled
groundnut oil for deep-frying
sea salt flakes
4 x 450g (1lb) freshly cooked lobsters
(see page 11)

FOR THE GARLIC BUTTER
170g (6oz) unsalted butter, cubed
3 fat garlic cloves, crushed
30ml (2 tablespoons) chopped fresh flat-leaf parsley
juice of ¼ lemon
salt and freshly ground black pepper

❍ Cut the potatoes to your desired thickness and wash in cold water. Place in a bowl of cold water and leave to stand for 10 minutes. Drain and dry thoroughly with a clean tea towel.

❍ Pour enough oil for deep-frying into a deep frying pan. Heat to about 165°C (330°F) before adding the chips. Blanch the chips first in the oil for 4–5 minutes, then remove from the oil (the chips should just yield to the touch). Heat the oil to about 195°C (385°F), add the chips and cook for 5–8 minutes to crisp and turn golden brown. Using a slotted spoon, transfer the chips to kitchen paper to drain and season with sea salt.

❍ Meanwhile, pre-heat a charcoal grill or ridged cast-iron grill pan on the hob until hot. Split the lobsters in half lengthways and crack the claws with the back of the knife. Place the split lobsters, shell-side down, on the grill or grill pan and cook for 5–8 minutes, turning once.

❍ Meanwhile, melt the butter in a small pan, add the garlic, parsley, lemon juice and seasoning and cook for 2 minutes.

❍ Divide the lobsters among 4 serving plates and spoon the garlic butter over them. Serve the chips separately.

Pesce San Pietro all'Uvetta

John Dory with Orvieto Sauce and Grapes

While the cooking technique lends itself perfectly to this delicious fish, unfortunately its price makes it less accessible for everyday meals, as you don't get much for your money. However, I think its taste is worth every penny.

SERVES 4
PREPARATION TIME: 30 MINUTES
COOKING TIME: 30 MINUTES

170g (6oz) butter, diced
4 x 225g (8oz) John Dory fillets, pin-boned
(see page 10)
4 shallots, finely chopped
150ml (5fl oz) Orvieto wine
15ml (1 tablespoon) double cream

340g (12oz) white seedless grapes, halved
340g (12oz) baby spinach, washed and drained
salt and freshly ground black pepper

FOR THE MASHED POTATOES
900g (2lb) Maris Piper potatoes, scrubbed clean
90ml (6 tablespoons) crème fraîche
55g (2oz) butter
freshly grated nutmeg, to taste

❍ Prick the potatoes with a skewer or fork, place in a large pan of salted water and bring to the boil. Cook for 15–20 minutes until tender. Drain, and when cool enough to handle, peel the potatoes and mash in a large bowl with a potato masher. Stir in the crème fraîche, 30g (1oz) of the butter and the nutmeg. Season to taste.

❍ Meanwhile, pre-heat the oven to 200°C/400°F/Gas Mark 6. Grease a baking tray with a little butter.

❍ Place the fish fillets on the baking tray, then sprinkle the shallots and 15ml (1 tablespoon) of the wine over them. Cover the fish with buttered greaseproof paper, then with foil, and bake for 7–9 minutes until the fish is tender.

❍ Carefully pour the juices from the John Dory into a pan and keep the fish warm. Place the pan on the hob, add the remaining wine and bring to the boil. Boil rapidly to reduce by half. Stir in the cream, then gradually whisk in 170g (6oz) diced butter. Stir in 225g (8oz) of grapes and season to taste.

❍ Melt the remaining 30g (1oz) of butter in a frying pan and, when foaming, add the spinach. Sauté for 3 minutes until just wilted. Season to taste.

❍ Place the mashed potatoes on 4 warmed serving plates and spoon the spinach next to the potatoes. Top the spinach with a fish fillet and spoon the sauce over it, scattering the remaining grapes over and around the fish. Sprinkle with extra black pepper and serve immediately.

Sogliola Limanda al Cartoccio

Lemon Sole Baked in Herbs and Rice Paper

Chinese rice paper is available at specialist Chinese food shops and some large supermarkets. However, it must not be confused with baking rice paper – they are completely different. This rice paper is used as a wrapping for ingredients, and then the whole parcel is deep-fried and eaten.
Accompany this dish with a tomato and basil salad.

SERVES 4
PREPARATION TIME: 30 MINUTES
COOKING TIME: 15–20 MINUTES

30g (1oz) fresh flat-leaf parsley
675g (1½lb) lemon sole fillets, skinned and trimmed
grated zest and juice of 1 lime
30ml (2 tablespoons) plain flour
30ml (2 tablespoons) water
12 large circles of Chinese rice paper
2 plum tomatoes, peeled and thinly sliced
(see page 26)

90ml (6 tablespoons) sunflower oil
salt and freshly ground black pepper

FOR THE TOMATO AND BASIL SALAD
675g (1½lb) ripe plum tomatoes, skinned, seeded
and roughly chopped (see page 26)
12 fresh basil leaves, roughly torn
30ml (2 tablespoons) capers, drained
30ml (2 tablespoons) extra virgin olive oil
15ml (1 tablespoon) good balsamic vinegar
salt and freshly ground black pepper

○ Gather the parsley into a bunch, hold it by its stems and plunge the leaves in boiling water for 30 seconds. Rinse the parsley in cold water and pat dry with kitchen paper. Remove the leaves from the stems.

○ Cut the fish into 7.5cm (3in) squares and sprinkle with the lime zest and juice and season with salt and pepper.

○ Mix together the flour and water to form a paste. Dip one rice paper circle in hot water for 30 seconds until it is floppy, then cool it in cold water. Place a few parsley leaves in the centre of the circle, top with a slice of tomato, then top with fish. Season to taste. Brush the rice paper edges with the flour paste and fold over first one side and then the other like an envelope to enclose the fish completely. Repeat, only using one rice paper circle at a time, to make 12 parcels in total.

○ Heat the sunflower oil in a large heavy-based pan. Working in batches, place 3–4 fish parcels in the pan, folded-side up, and cook for 3 minutes. Turn over and cook for a further 2 minutes until the rice paper is golden brown. Drain on kitchen paper and keep warm while cooking the remaining fish parcels.

○ Meanwhile, mix together the tomatoes, basil, capers, olive oil and vinegar. Season to taste.

○ Place 3 fish parcels on each plate and surround with the tomato and basil salad. Serve immediately.

Triglia della Nonna

Red Mullet with Fresh Tomatoes, Garlic and Fennel Seeds

Red mullet is a great Mediterranean fish but not one of the most popular because it has a lot of small bones. It therefore takes more time to eat but the reward is a fantastic flavour. When barbecuing, try cooking the whole fish and serving it with a mixed salad. *Della Nonna* means that it's Grandma's recipe.

SERVES 4
PREPARATION TIME: 20 MINUTES
COOKING TIME: 35 MINUTES

60ml (4 tablespoons) extra virgin olive oil
15ml (1 tablespoon) fennel seeds
4 garlic cloves, sliced
1 onion, finely chopped
450g (1lb) plum tomatoes, roughly cut into large chunks

1 fennel bulb, trimmed and sliced lengthways
4 x 225–340g (8–12oz) whole red mullets, cleaned and scaled (see page 10)
4 large sprigs of fresh thyme
1 lemon, thinly sliced
salt and freshly ground black pepper
30ml (2 tablespoons) chopped fresh flat-leaf parsley, to serve

❍ Pre-heat the oven to 200°C/400°F/Gas Mark 6.

❍ Heat a frying pan over a low heat, then add half of the oil. Add the fennel seeds, cover and remove from the heat. Leave for 1 minute – the seeds should be golden brown.

❍ Reduce the heat, return the pan to the hob and stir in the garlic and onion. Cook for 3–5 minutes until soft but not browned. Stir in the tomatoes and cook for 5 minutes. Season to taste.

❍ Meanwhile, bring a separate pan of salted water to the boil, add the sliced fennel and blanch for 2 minutes. Drain.

❍ Pour the tomato mixture into a large roasting tin or ovenproof gratin dish and gently mix in the blanched fennel.

❍ Pat the red mullets dry and season all over the outside and inside of the fish. Put the thyme sprigs and lemon slices inside the fish, then place the fish on the top of the tomatoes and drizzle with the remaining oil. Bake for 15–20 minutes until the fish is tender. Sprinkle with parsley and serve immediately.

Nasello in Salsa Verde

Poached Hake in Green Pickle Sauce

Hake is inexpensive and in my opinion very under-rated. As the bone is triangular in shape it is quite easy to remove when cooked through properly. In fact, you can use a whole 1.6kg (3½lb) hake for this recipe, if preferred. My mother used to cook it with first-pressed olive oil – pure olive oil which is very strong in flavour, with a slight bitterness. Flavoured with green pickle sauce (salsa verde), this lovely summer recipe is perfect served with simple vegetables such as boiled potatoes and beans. Alternatively, this recipe can be served with plain cooked pasta.

SERVES 4
PREPARATION TIME: 10 MINUTES
COOKING TIME: 5–8 MINUTES

900ml (1½ pints) Court Bouillon (see page 165)
4 x 170–225g (6–8oz) hake steaks

FOR THE GREEN PICKLE SAUCE
6 small gherkins
30ml (2 tablespoons) capers in salt, rinsed and
patted dry with kitchen paper

1 fresh green chilli, seeded and finely chopped
1 shallot, diced
60ml (4 tablespoons) chopped fresh flat-leaf parsley
12 fresh basil leaves, torn
15ml (1 tablespoon) chopped fresh dill
grated zest of 1 lime
90ml (6 tablespoons) extra virgin olive oil
salt and freshly ground black pepper

○ Pour the court bouillon into a large frying pan and add the fish. Gently bring to a simmer and poach for 3–4 minutes (time from when the liquid comes to a simmer) until the fish is tender. Drain the fish and pat dry with kitchen paper.

○ Meanwhile, put the gherkins, capers and chilli in a food processor and process for 30 seconds. Add the remaining ingredients except the oil. Process again, this time gradually pouring in the oil to combine thoroughly.

○ Arrange the fish on 4 warmed serving plates and spoon the green pickle sauce over it. Serve immediately.

Mosaico di Pesci

Mosaic of Mixed Fish

This idea is based on the traditional Italian recipe, bollito misto where a variety of meats are boiled. Here the fish adds a much lighter and healthier touch. For extra flavour serve with pesto. Steamed new potatoes with mint will make a superb accompaniment.

SERVES 4
PREPARATION TIME: 30 MINUTES
COOKING TIME: 55 MINUTES

125g (4½oz) butter
4 x 85g (3oz) salmon fillets
4 x 85g (3oz) turbot fillets
4 x 85g (3oz) monkfish fillets
4 langoustines
juice of 2 lemons
5ml (1 teaspoon) sea salt

5ml (1 teaspoon) freshly ground black pepper
30ml (2 tablespoons) extra virgin olive oil
4 sprigs of fresh flat-leaf parsley, to garnish

FOR THE COURT BOUILLON
1 litre (1¾ pints) water
150ml (5fl oz) dry white wine
1 red onion, sliced
4 celery sticks
4 bay leaves
4 fresh sprigs of fresh rosemary

❍ Make a court bouillon in a large pan with the water, wine, vegetables and herbs (see page 164). Bring to the boil, simmer for 30 minutes, then strain through muslin.

❍ Pre-heat the oven to 180°C/350°F/Gas Mark 4. Using some of the butter, lightly grease an ovenproof dish large enough to hold all of the fish in a single layer.

❍ Arrange all of the fish and the langoustines in the dish and ladle over the court bouillon to half cover the fish. Cover with buttered greaseproof paper, then with foil. Poach in the oven for 20 minutes until all the fish are tender.

❍ Remove the paper and foil, then gently transfer the fish to 4 large serving plates, placing a langoustine on top of each one. Strain the court bouillon through a fine sieve and return it to the pan. Boil for 5 minutes to reduce it by half. Remove from the heat and stir in the remaining butter, lemon juice and seasoning. Divide the sauce among the fish, drizzle with the oil and garnish with the parsley sprigs. Serve immediately.

Family
Meals &
Roasts

Rombo al Forno

Whole Roast Turbot

This fish brings back memories of early morning trips to the fish market because it's not as easy to find as salmon and tuna. It's well worth rising at dawn because when turbot is bought fresh and cooked this way, it's simply delicious. It needs very little work – just add fresh, good quality ingredients.

Turbot is a flat fish with firm flesh; its fine taste makes it perfect for poaching and serving with some new-season spring vegetables. This roast turbot recipe is more robust and can be served with roasted potatoes and caramelized carrots. It is an easy fish to take off the bone so serve the whole fish if you like.

SERVES 4
PREPARATION TIME: 30 MINUTES
COOKING TIME: 35 MINUTES

1 x 1.8kg (4lb) turbot, cleaned, washed and patted dry
2 fat garlic cloves, crushed
15ml (1 tablespoon) chopped fresh thyme leaves
15ml (1 tablespoon) chopped fresh rosemary leaves
60ml (4 tablespoons) extra virgin olive oil

FOR THE VEGETABLE GARNISH
24 shallots
170g (6oz) pancetta, cut into batons
225g (8oz) button mushrooms, trimmed
170g (6oz) unsalted butter, diced and chilled
30ml (2 tablespoons) chopped fresh flat-leaf parsley
salt and freshly ground black pepper

❍ Pre-heat the oven to 200°C/400°F/Gas Mark 6.

❍ Season the turbot inside and out and rub with the garlic. Place the fish in a large roasting tin, dark skin down, sprinkle the chopped thyme and rosemary over it, drizzle with a little oil and roast for 30 minutes.

❍ Meanwhile, divide the remaining oil among 3 separate pans, place over a high heat and add the shallots, pancetta and mushrooms separately to each pan. Cook the mushrooms for about 3 minutes, the pancetta for 3–5 minutes until crisp and the shallots for about 10 minutes.

❍ Remove the fish from the tin and place on a large platter. Cover with foil and keep warm. Place the tin over a gentle heat on the hob, add all of the vegetables and the butter and stir until the butter melts into the pan juices. Stir in the chopped parsley and spoon directly over the turbot. Serve the fish immediately.

Guazzetto di Rana Pescatrice

Monkfish in Tomato and Basil Sauce

The simple combination of tomato and basil is my favourite. I like adapting this combination when cooking fish, but you could also serve this dish simply with roasted tomatoes and extra virgin olive oil. Accompany with a bitter leaf salad.
To toast the pine nuts for the garnish, heat 15ml (1 tablespoon) of olive oil in a frying pan, add the nuts and toast for 1–2 minutes over a medium heat.

SERVES 4
PREPARATION TIME: 10 MINUTES
COOKING TIME: 35 MINUTES

4 x 170g (6oz) monkfish fillets, cleaned and patted dry with kitchen paper
120ml (8 tablespoons) extra virgin olive oil

FOR THE TOMATO AND BASIL SAUCE
1 small onion, finely chopped
2 garlic cloves, finely chopped

250g (9oz) cherry tomatoes, halved
85g (3oz) sun-dried tomatoes in oil, drained
1 sprig of fresh rosemary
30g (1oz) fresh basil, stalks discarded and leaves torn
150ml (5fl oz) dry white wine
150ml (5fl oz) Fish Stock (see page 164)
salt and freshly ground black pepper
30g (1oz) pine nuts, toasted, to garnish

❍ Pre-heat the oven to 200°C/400°F/Gas Mark 6.

❍ Place the fish on a large platter and brush well with 30ml (2 tablespoons) of the oil – this is to make sure that the fish does not stick on cooking.

❍ Place a large roasting tin on the hob and add the remaining oil. Heat until hot, then stir in the onion. Cook for 5 minutes until golden. Stir in the garlic, cherry tomatoes, sun-dried tomatoes, rosemary and half of the basil and cook for a further 5 minutes.

❍ Make room for the fish in the centre of the roasting tin, add the fish and cook for 3 minutes, turning several times to seal all over. Add the wine and half of the stock and season to taste.

❍ Transfer the roasting tin to the oven and cook for 15–20 minutes until the fish is tender – check if it's cooked by piercing it with a skewer and if it comes out hot then it is ready to serve. Add extra stock if the roasting tin seems dry during cooking.

❍ Spoon the sauce on to a large platter and arrange the fish on top. Sprinkle with the remaining basil and pine nuts and serve immediately.

Arrosto Misto di Pesce

Roast Mixed Fish

This is a very simple and cheat's way of making Fritto Misto (see page 14) and it's also much healthier!

This herb crust is also a good mixture to coat large fillets of fish before baking – simply coat the fish in seasoned flour, dip it in egg, then coat with the breadcrumbs.

SERVES 4
PREPARATION TIME: 25 MINUTES
COOKING TIME: 10–15 MINUTES

FOR THE HERB BREADCRUMBS
170g (6oz) fresh breadcrumbs made from focaccia or ciabatta bread
15g (½oz) pine nuts
1 fat garlic clove, crushed
8 fresh leaves basil, torn
30ml (2 tablespoons) chopped fresh flat-leaf parsley
salt and freshly ground black pepper

FOR THE SEAFOOD
125g (4½oz) tuna fillet
125g (4½oz) salmon fillet
4 raw king prawns
125g (4½oz) monkfish fillet
125g (4½oz) swordfish fillet
125g (4½oz) red snapper fillet
45ml (3 tablespoons) extra virgin olive oil
lemon wedges, to serve

○ Pre-heat the oven to 200°C/400°F/Gas Mark 6.

○ Place all the ingredients for the breadcrumbs into a food processor and process for about 1 minute, then season to taste. Place in a shallow plate.

○ Prepare the fish, ensuring that they are free from bones, and split each piece except the king prawns into 4 pieces. Drizzle 15ml (1 tablespoon) of the oil over a baking tray large enough to hold all the fish when laid out flat. Season to taste, drizzle a little more oil over the seafood and sprinkle with the breadcrumb mixture.

○ Roast the fish for 10–15 minutes until just tender, golden and crisp. Transfer the fish to a large platter and drizzle with the remaining oil. Serve with the lemon wedges.

Tortine di Salmone e Merluzzo

Salmon and Cod Fish Cakes

This is a great kid's recipe and one of my daughter's favourites. It's also a first choice for all my office staff. I like to serve this with big fat chips and Tartare Sauce (pages 128 and 167), or you can try a light salad, Red Pepper Salsa (see page 171) and lemon wedges.

SERVES 4
PREPARATION TIME: 15 MINUTES
COOKING TIME: 25 MINUTES

450g (1lb) potatoes, scrubbed clean
675g (1½lb) mixed salmon and cod fillets, skinned
900ml (1½ pints) Court Bouillon (see page 165)
125g (4½oz) butter

1 garlic clove, finely chopped
15ml (1 tablespoon) chopped fresh tarragon
15ml (1 tablespoon) chopped fresh chives
5ml (1 teaspoon) salt
5ml (1 teaspoon) white pepper
15ml (1 tablespoon) plain flour
150ml (5fl oz) extra virgin olive oil

❍ Put the potatoes in a large pan of salted water and bring to the boil. Cook for 15 minutes until tender. Drain and leave to cool.

❍ Meanwhile, put the fish in a large frying pan and pour in the court bouillon. Bring to the boil, then reduce the heat and poach for 10 minutes. Drain and flake the fish, discarding the skin and removing any bones.

❍ When cool enough to handle, peel the potatoes and mash them in a large bowl with the butter, garlic, tarragon, chives and seasoning. Mix in the fish flakes. Divide the mixture into 4 and, using your hands, shape into patties, then dust on all sides with flour.

❍ Heat the oil in a large shallow frying pan and add the fish cakes. Cook for 3–4 minutes on each side until golden brown. Using a slotted spoon, transfer to kitchen paper to drain. Serve immediately.

Calamari Ripieni in Casseruola

Stuffed Squid Casserole

Good Italian sausages are only available from delis as far as I'm concerned – these are not the salami style. These sausages need to be cooked and, unlike British sausages, they are full of spices and lots of meat. As well as being used for stuffings, they are often boiled and the liquid is turned into a broth for bean stews – the flavours that come out of them just cannot be wasted!

Look out for the fresh Napoletana sauces now available in the chilled cabinets in supermarkets.

SERVES 4
PREPARATION TIME: 45 MINUTES
COOKING TIME: 35 MINUTES

8 medium-sized squid, cleaned (see page 12)
150ml (5fl oz) dry white wine
1.2 litres (2 pints) ready-made Napoletana sauce
salt and freshly ground black pepper
cooked saffron rice, to serve

FOR THE STUFFING
450g (1lb) Italian sausages
30ml (2 tablespoons) extra virgin olive oil
3 large baking potatoes, peeled and finely diced
2 garlic cloves, finely chopped
30g (1oz) fresh basil, stalks discarded and leaves finely chopped
30ml (2 tablespoons) chopped sun-dried tomatoes
30ml (2 tablespoons) dried breadcrumbs
juice of ½ lemon

❍ Pre-heat the oven to 200°C/400°F/Gas Mark 6.

❍ Peel the skins from the sausages and discard. Put the sausage meat in a large bowl and break up. Heat the oil in a large frying pan, add the sausage meat and fry for 2 minutes. Stir in the potatoes and garlic and cook for a further 3 minutes. Transfer the mixture to a bowl and mix in the basil, tomatoes and breadcrumbs. Add the lemon juice and season.

❍ Pat the squid dry with kitchen paper, then spoon the stuffing into each cavity and secure with a wooden cocktail stick. Put the squid in an ovenproof gratin dish with the tentacles, pour the wine and Napoletana sauce over it and cover with foil. Bake for 30 minutes until the squid are tender.

❍ Spoon the rice into the centre of 4 warmed serving plates. Remove and discard the cocktail sticks from the squid. Halve each squid lengthways and arrange 4 halves on each plate. Spoon the sauce over the squid and serve immediately with rice.

Nasello all'Abruzzese

Roast Hake with Rosemary and Breadcrumbs

Roast fish, like roast meat, is complete served with roasted vegetables such as courgettes, peppers, aubergines and spring onions. Simply prepare the vegetables and sprinkle with extra virgin olive oil, balsamic vinegar, garlic and rosemary sprigs. Add a little sea salt flakes and freshly ground black pepper and cook for 30–40 minutes until very soft and a little charred.

SERVES 4
PREPARATION TIME: 15 MINUTES
COOKING TIME: 35 MINUTES

1kg (2¼lb) hake, cleaned
1 large sprig of fresh rosemary
120ml (4fl oz) extra virgin olive oil
2 garlic cloves, finely chopped
30ml (2 tablespoons) finely chopped fresh
rosemary leaves

4 bay leaves
30g (1oz) fresh breadcrumbs made from
focaccia bread
salt and freshly ground black pepper

TO SERVE
roasted vegetables
lime wedges

❍ Pre-heat the oven to 160°C/325°F/Gas Mark 3.

❍ Season the hake inside and out, put the rosemary sprig inside and season again. Place the fish in a lightly greased ovenproof dish.

❍ Heat 90ml (3fl oz) of the oil in a pan over a low heat. Add the garlic and cook for 3 minutes until golden brown. Remove from the heat and pour over the hake, making sure some of it drizzles inside the fish. Place the rosemary and the bay leaves on top of the fish and sprinkle with the breadcrumbs. Roast for 30 minutes. If the breadcrumb crust appears to be getting too dry, drizzle the remaining oil over it. The fish should be very tender. (For an extra-crisp top, put the fish under a pre-heated hot grill for 2 minutes.)

❍ Serve the roasted fish directly from the roasting tin with roasted mixed vegetables and lime wedges.

Spigola al Sale

Whole Sea Bass in Salt and Pepper Crust

When I recently visited Portugal for a holiday with my family, we frequently ate this dish. I think it's brilliant for a dinner party because it's so simple. Serve it as part of a four course meal. I prefer to let everyone dress their own fish for dinner – its so much more fun!

SERVES 6
PREPARATION TIME: 20 MINUTES
COOKING TIME: 20–25 MINUTES

2kg (4½lb) sea bass, gutted and gilled only
(see page 10)

FOR THE CRUST
900g (2lb) coarse sea salt
170g (6oz) mixed peppercorns
2 egg whites

FOR THE DRESSING
175ml (6fl oz) extra virgin olive oil
60ml (4 tablespoons) fresh lemon juice
2 lemons, thickly sliced
90ml (6 tablespoons) roughly chopped fresh
flat-leaf parsley
freshly ground black pepper

❍ Pre-heat the oven to 200°C/400°F/Gas Mark 6. Pat the fish dry with kitchen paper.

❍ Mix together the sea salt, peppercorns and egg whites. Spread a little of the salt crust mixture on a baking tray large enough for the fish and place the fish on top. Press the remaining crust all over to completely enclose the fish. Roast for 20–25 minutes.

❍ Meanwhile, mix the oil, lemon juice and black pepper in a small bowl (you don't need salt as the fish is already well seasoned). Heat a heavy-based frying pan until very hot and cook the lemon slices for 2–3 minutes on each side until browned. Place the parsley in another bowl.

❍ As soon as you remove the fish from the oven, break the salt crust and lift off. If the skin does not come off with the crust, gently peel it away. Open out half of the fish and lift out the bones – don't worry if the fillets break up. Arrange the fish on a large platter and serve with the lemon dressing, parsley and cooked lemons for your guests to dress their own fish. Alternatively, dress it for them on individual plates.

Tonno al Pepe

Peppered Roast Loin of Tuna

Here a loin of tuna is treated very much like fillet steak. Tuna has a good strong flavour and can easily handle the pungent peppercorns; keep the cooking to a minimum. To complete the meal, boil some new potatoes until slightly underdone, then transfer to a roasting tin with some baby carrots, drizzle with extra virgin olive oil and a touch of honey, then sprinkle with crushed peppercorns and sea salt flakes. Roast for 10 minutes until tender.

SERVES 4
PREPARATION TIME: 10 MINUTES
COOKING TIME: 10 MINUTES PLUS
5 MINUTES RESTING

450g (1lb) piece tuna fillet
30ml (2 tablespoons) extra virgin olive oil
15 (1 tablespoon) smooth Dijon mustard
30ml (2 tablespoons) mixed peppercorns, roughly crushed

FOR THE SAUCE
15ml (1 tablespoon) balsamic vinegar
150ml (5fl oz) Fish Stock (see page 164)
5ml (1 teaspoon) clear honey
salt and freshly ground black pepper

❍ Pre-heat the oven to 200°C/400°F/Gas Mark 6.

❍ Brush the tuna with a little of the oil, then spread the mustard all over. Roll the tuna in the peppercorns to coat.

❍ Heat a large heavy-based frying pan until hot, then add the remaining oil and heat until hot. Add the tuna and cook for 3 minutes, turning constantly to seal all over. Wrap the tuna in foil, place on a baking tray and roast for 7 minutes – the tuna should still be rare in the centre. Allow to rest for 5 minutes still wrapped in the foil.

❍ Meanwhile, add the vinegar to the pan juices and cook, stirring, for 30 seconds to deglaze the pan. Stir in the stock and cook for 5 minutes until reduced by one-third. Stir in the honey and season to taste. Cook for 2 minutes until syrupy.

❍ Thinly slice the tuna, arrange on a warmed serving plate and spoon the sauce over it. Serve immediately.

Trota di Mare Arrosto

Baked Sea Trout

Sea trout is very much like salmon in that both have a pink skin and sweet taste. Trout is another fish which is extremely versatile. I also love to bake river trout and then marinate it with onions, vinegar, olive oil and herbs and leave it in the fridge overnight. This recipe will give you loads of time to socialize with dinner guests while the fish is baking.

SERVES 4
PREPARATION TIME: 30 MINUTES
COOKING TIME: 30 MINUTES

1 x 1.4kg (3lb) sea trout, cleaned
8 black peppercorns, roughly crushed
3 sprigs of fresh thyme
1 stick of lemon grass, gently bruised
2.5cm (1in) piece of fresh root ginger, peeled and sliced
4 garlic cloves, sliced

30ml (2 tablespoons) extra virgin olive oil
1 x 675g (1½lb) butternut squash, peeled and cut into 2.5cm (1in) chunks
340g (12oz) sweet potatoes, peeled and cut into 2.5cm (1in) chunks
grated zest and juice of 2 limes
150ml (5fl oz) Fish Stock (see page 164)
90ml (4 tablespoons) chopped fresh coriander leaves
salt and freshly ground black pepper
extra virgin olive oil, to drizzle

❍ Pre-heat the oven to 180°C/350°F/Gas Mark 4.

❍ Pat the sea trout dry with kitchen paper and season inside and out. Fill the inside with the peppercorns, thyme, lemon grass, ginger and garlic.

❍ Pour half of the oil into a large roasting tin, add the fish and surround with the butternut squash and sweet potatoes. Sprinkle the fish and vegetables with the lime zest and juice then season the vegetables to taste. Pour the stock over the fish and vegetables and drizzle with the remaining oil. Cover with foil and bake for 30 minutes, stirring the vegetables after 20 minutes, until the fish and vegetables are tender.

❍ Sprinkle the fish and vegetables with the coriander, drizzle with a little oil and serve straight from the roasting tin.

Zuppa di Pesce

Traditional Italian Fish Stew

Fish stew does not sound like a fantastic dish, but this is only because of the name;
in French it sounds so wonderful – bouillabaisse. This is the perfect alternative
Sunday lunch. The selection of fish you use is entirely up to you – try adding salmon and
cod too if you like.
Serve with a nice chilled Abruzzo rosé wine called Campirosa Montepulciano d'Abruzzo.

SERVES 4
PREPARATION TIME: 45 MINUTES PLUS
30 MINUTES SOAKING
COOKING TIME: 40 MINUTES

340g (12oz) mussels
340g (12oz) clams
675g (1½lb) red mullet, cleaned and filleted (ask
the fishmonger for the fish bones)
200ml (7fl oz) water
4 langoustines
8 raw jumbo prawns
salt and freshly ground black pepper
crusty bread or Garlic and Olive Oil Toast
(see page 175)

FOR THE STEW BASE
45ml (3 tablespoons) extra virgin olive oil
4 garlic cloves, chopped
3 sprigs of fresh thyme
2 bay leaves, torn
1 strip of orange zest
1 large onion, chopped
1 x 0.125g sachet saffron powder or a good pinch
of saffron strands
2 small dried chillies, crushed
1 stick celery, trimmed and chopped
2 baby fennel bulbs, chopped
½ yellow pepper, seeded and chopped
2 carrots, chopped
1 beef tomato, roughly chopped
150ml (5fl oz) dry white wine
600ml (1 pint) cold water

❍ Scrub the mussels clean and remove the beards and barnacles. Soak the clams in salted water for 30 minutes to remove the grit, then wash in clean water and drain.

❍ Heat the oil in a large heavy-based deep pan and add the garlic, thyme, bay leaves and orange zest. Cook for 30 seconds, then add the onion, cover and cook for 5 minutes until the onion softens. Stir in the saffron, chillies, celery, fennel and yellow pepper, cover and cook for a further 3 minutes. Add the carrots, cover and cook for a further 5 minutes.

❍ Roughly cut up the fish bones and add to the pan. Reduce the heat and mash the bones with a wooden spoon. Add the tomato and wine, increase the heat to high and boil for 3 minutes. Pour 600ml (1 pint) water into the pan, bring to the boil and cook for 5 minutes. Remove and discard the thyme sprigs, bay leaves and orange zest.

❍ Working in batches, process the stew base in a food processor, then pass it through a fine sieve and return it to the pan. Season to taste. Set aside.

○ Place the mussels and 50ml (2fl oz) water in a large heavy-based deep pan. Cover tightly and cook over a high heat for 3–5 minutes, shaking the pan frequently, until the shells have opened. Transfer the mussels to a large bowl. Add the clams to the pan, cover and cook for 3–5 minutes until opened. Add the clams to the mussels. Add the langoustines and prawns to the pan, cover and cook for 3 minutes until bright pink. Transfer the langoustines and prawns to the stew base.

○ Add 150ml (5fl oz) of cold water to the pan juices and bring to the boil. Gently add the red mullet fillets and poach for 3 minutes until just tender. Lift the fish out and set aside. Boil the pan juices for 2 minutes, then strain and add to the stew.

○ Discard any mussels and clams that have remained closed, then shell half of each. Add the shelled mussels and clams to the stew. Pile the remaining mussels and clams in a large serving bowl and top with the poached fish. Reheat the stew and ladle over the fish, arranging the prawns and langoustines in the bowl. Serve immediately with crusty bread or garlic and olive oil toast.

Cozze e Patate allo Zafferano

Mussel and Potato Hot Pot with Saffron

Mussels can be cooked in a variety of ways, but with saffron they have a lovely colour and beautiful flavour. Make sure you have a chilled bottle of Italian Chardonnay ready to serve with this delicious dish.

SERVES 4
PREPARATION TIME: 25 MINUTES
COOKING TIME: 20 MINUTES

450g (1lb) new potatoes, scrubbed
30ml (2 tablespoons) extra virgin olive oil
4 shallots, finely sliced
2 bay leaves
2 sprigs of fresh thyme
a good pinch of saffron strands
2 garlic cloves, finely chopped
900g (2lb) mussels, scrubbed clean, beards and barnacles removed
150ml (5fl oz) dry white wine
2 beef tomatoes, peeled, seeded and diced (see page 26)
300ml (10fl oz) double cream
60ml (4 tablespoons) chopped fresh flat-leaf parsley
salt and freshly ground black pepper

❍ Put the potatoes in a large pan of salted water and bring to the boil. Cook for 12–15 minutes until tender.

❍ Meanwhile, heat the oil in a separate large heavy-based deep pan until hot. Add the shallots, bay leaves, thyme and saffron and cook for 2 minutes. Add the garlic, then stir in the mussels and white wine. Cover the pan tightly and cook, shaking the pan frequently, for 3–5 minutes over a high heat until the shells have opened. Transfer the mussels to a large bowl. Discard any mussels that have remained closed. Set aside.

❍ Strain the pan juices, then return them to a clean pan and boil until reduced by one-half. Add the tomatoes, cream, potatoes and parsley. Heat through and season to taste.

❍ Divide the mussels among 4 large warmed bowls and spoon the potatoes and juices over them. Serve immediately.

The Zilli Fish Experience

Crostacei alle Tre Maionesi

Crustacea with Three Mayonnaise Dips

This is a real family treat. Serve the ready-prepared shellfish on a big platter, on crushed ice, with a little seaweed to decorate and plenty of crispy bread; finger bowls and napkins are essential. The three mayonnaise dips – classic mayonnaise, anchovy and caper and rouille – are all traditional fish accompaniments.

SERVES 6
PREPARATION TIME: 30 MINUTES

FOR THE MAYONNAISE
240ml (8fl oz) olive oil
240ml (8fl oz) sunflower oil
3 medium egg yolks
45ml (3 tablespoons) fresh lemon juice
5ml (1 teaspoon) Dijon mustard
grated zest and juice of 1 lemon (optional)
6 garlic cloves, crushed
30ml (2 tablespoons) capers, chopped
12 anchovy fillets, finely chopped
5ml (1 teaspoon) tomato purée
60ml (4 tablespoons) finely chopped peeled red peppers (see page 171)
cayenne pepper, to taste
salt and freshly ground black pepper

FOR THE SHELLFISH PLATTER
225g (8oz) samphire, washed
4 cooked langoustines
4 cooked green-lipped New Zealand mussels
8 cooked king prawns, tails peeled
6 oysters, scrubbed clean and shucked
450g (1lb) cooked prawns
225g (8oz) winkles
6 cooked queen scallops in half shells
1 medium-size dressed crab

TO SERVE
4 lemons, halved
sea salt flakes and freshly ground black pepper

❍ Make the mayonnaise either in a blender or by hand (see page 166). To make it in a blender, mix together the olive and sunflower oils. Put the egg yolks, 45ml (3 tablespoons) lemon juice and the mustard in a blender and season well to taste. Blend while gradually adding the mixed oils in a steady stream until the mayonnaise is thick.

❍ Divide the mayonnaise among 3 bowls. Leave one as it is or add the juice and zest of another lemon for lemon mayonnaise. To the second add one-third of the garlic and all of the capers and anchovy fillets. To the third, beat in the tomato purée, red peppers and remaining garlic and cayenne pepper to taste. Chill the dips until required.

❍ Bring a large pan of water to the boil, add the samphire and blanch for 1 minute. Drain and refresh under cold water. Drain well.

❍ Fill 1–2 large platters with roughly crushed ice. Arrange the shellfish on the platters and garnish with the samphire. Serve immediately with the 3 mayonnaises, the lemon halves and plenty of sea salt and black pepper.

Lombo di Pesce Spada al Rosmarino

Roast Loin of Swordfish with Rosemary and Garlic

Like tuna, swordfish has become widely available over the last few years. Swordfish steaks are also great – you can use this same method, just reduce the cooking time to 15 minutes and keep a careful eye on them as they can become too dry if overcooked.

I remember when we cooked this dish to test it for quantities, the smells in the kitchen were mesmerizing; I sat down in my restaurant, Signor Zilli, to eat it for lunch – the first customers that came in that day wanted the same!

SERVES 4
PREPARATION TIME: 20 MINUTES
COOKING TIME: 40 MINUTES

1.25kg (2¾lb) loin of swordfish
6 garlic cloves
15g (½oz) fresh oregano
30g (1oz) fresh rosemary, broken into small sprigs

30ml (2 tablespoons) extra virgin olive oil
15ml (1 tablespoon) sea salt
15ml (1 tablespoon) plain flour

TO SERVE
sautéed green beans
rocket and Parmesan cheese salad

❍ Pre-heat the oven to 225°C/425°F/Gas Mark 7.

❍ Pat the swordfish dry with kitchen paper. Using a sharp knife, make 6 cuts in the fish. Crush 3 unpeeled garlic cloves with a knife, then cut them in half; put ½ clove in each cut with some of the sprigs of oregano and rosemary.

❍ Peel the remaining garlic cloves and finely chop. Remove the leaves from the remaining oregano and rosemary and finely chop.

❍ Heat the oil in a large heavy-based pan. Rub the fish with the sea salt and dust with some flour. Place the fish in the pan and cook for 2 minutes on each side. Cover with the chopped garlic, oregano and rosemary and wrap in a piece of foil. Place the fish on a baking tray and roast for 35 minutes.

❍ Remove the fish from the oven and then remove the foil, reserving any juices. (If the fish is still a little rare, quickly finish it off under a pre-heated medium-hot grill for 2 minutes.) Transfer the fish to a large serving platter and slice. Serve immediately with the sautéed green beans and the rocket and Parmesan cheese salad.

Aragosta Bellavista

Lobster in Orange and Chilli with Mustard Mashed Potatoes

A lobster doesn't need a lot of attention. It can be simply boiled, split open and served with mayonnaise and salad. If you're after something a bit more involved and with an adventurous taste, then this is the recipe you've been looking for.

SERVES 4
PREPARATION TIME: 40 MINUTES
COOKING TIME: 25 MINUTES

FOR THE MASHED POTATOES
4 large potatoes, washed
30ml (2 tablespoons) Dijon mustard
20ml (4 teaspoons) butter
10ml (2 teaspoons) double cream
5ml (1 teaspoon) freshly grated Parmesan cheese
salt and freshly ground black pepper

FOR THE LOBSTERS
4 x 450g (1lb) cooked lobsters
30g (1oz) butter
1 fresh red chilli, seeded and finely chopped
1 shallot, finely chopped
5ml (1 teaspoon) brown sugar
juice of 2 oranges
2 oranges, peeled and segmented
15ml (1 tablespoon) Grand Marnier

FOR THE GARNISH (OPTIONAL)
125g (4½oz) granulated sugar
1 orange, thinly sliced

○ Prick the potatoes with a skewer or fork, place in a pan of salted water and bring to the boil. Cook for 15–20 minutes until tender. Drain, and when cool enough to handle, peel the potatoes and mash in a large bowl with a potato masher. Stir in the mustard, butter, cream and Parmesan cheese and season to taste. Set aside and keep warm.

○ Meanwhile, cut the lobsters in half and remove the meat. Reserve the shells for presentation.

○ Melt the butter in a small pan, add the chilli and shallot and sauté for 5 minutes until tender but not brown. Add the brown sugar and orange juice and cook for 2–3 minutes until the sauce thickens.

○ Gently stir the lobster meat and orange segments into the sauce and cook for 3 minutes. Add the

Grand Marnier and season to taste. Simmer for a further minute.

○ If making the garnish, put the granulated sugar in a heavy-based pan and heat gently until the sugar dissolves, then cook for 2–3 minutes until the sugar turns to a golden caramel.

○ Meanwhile, pre-heat the grill to hot. Place the orange slices under the grill to dry out a little. Dip the orange slices in the caramel and set aside to set.

○ Fill the lobster shells with the mashed potatoes and place on hot serving plates. Spoon the lobster meat on to the mashed potatoes, then drizzle the sauce over the lobster. Garnish with the caramelized orange slices, if desired. Serve immediately.

Saltimbocca di Tonno

Tuna Escalope with Parma Ham and Sage

Saltimbocca is the traditional method of cooking veal with ham and fresh sage leaves, but I decided to use tuna instead and it works just as well if not better!
Tuna, like beef and lamb, is best served rare in the centre, therefore the minimum cooking time is required; if it's over-cooked, it's just too dry and unappetizing.
To complete the meal, serve the tuna with steamed baby carrots which have been pan-fried in a little butter, honey and lemon zest. Also offer new potatoes roasted with sea salt, plenty of freshly ground black pepper, whole unpeeled garlic cloves and sprigs of fresh rosemary – just perfect!

SERVES 4
PREPARATION TIME: 10 MINUTES
COOKING TIME: 7 MINUTES

4 x 125g (4½oz) thick tuna steaks
8 fresh sage leaves
4 thin slices Parma ham

30g (1oz) butter
150ml (5fl oz) dry white wine
15ml (1 tablespoon) finely chopped fresh flat-leaf parsley
juice of 1 lemon
salt and freshly ground black pepper
mizuna or rocket leaves, to garnish

❍ Pat the tuna steaks dry with kitchen paper and season all over. Place 1 sage leaf on each steak, then wrap a piece of Parma ham around each steak and secure with a wooden cocktail stick.

❍ Heat a large heavy-based frying pan, add the butter and heat until melted and frothy. Add the tuna steaks and cook for 2 minutes on each side until the ham turns a deep pink and begins to crisp in places. Remove the tuna and allow to rest for 2 minutes.

❍ Meanwhile, add the wine to the pan juices and boil for 2 minutes. Stir in the remaining sage leaves and parsley. Add the lemon juice and cook for 1 minute.

❍ Slice each piece of tuna into 3–4 pieces (the tuna should still be pink in the centre), arrange on serving plates and garnish with mizuna or rocket leaves. Spoon the sauce over the tuna and serve immediately.

Pinzimonio di Verdure all'Acciuga e Sarde

Crudités with Anchovy and Sardine Dip

This dip was specially devised for my Zilli Fish restaurant. Originally I used fresh anchovies, but the price kept going up, so we switched to sardines and it actually tastes better now!

SERVES 4
PREPARATION TIME: 20 MINUTES
COOKING TIME: 20 MINUTES

FOR THE DIP
4 sardines, filleted
1 x 50g (1¾oz) can anchovy fillets in oil
2 garlic cloves, finely chopped
2 sprigs of fresh flat-leaf parsley, roughly chopped
60ml (4 tablespoons) extra virgin olive oil
salt and freshly ground black pepper

FOR THE CRUDITÉS
2 large carrots
1 bunch spring onions, trimmed
1 cucumber, trimmed, quartered lengthways and seeded
1 red pepper, halved and seeded
125g (4½oz) baby courgettes, trimmed and quartered lengthways
125g (4½oz) baby corn, halved lengthways

❍ Pre-heat the oven to 200°C/400°F/Gas Mark 6.

❍ Put the sardines and anchovy fillets with their oil in an ovenproof dish, add the garlic and parsley and season to taste. Cover with foil and bake for 20 minutes until the sardines are very tender.

❍ Cool the sardines slightly, then place the sardine mixture in a food processor and process until smooth. Pass the purée through a sieve, then stir in the oil. Season to taste. Spoon the dip into 2 small serving bowls. Chill until serving.

❍ Cut the carrots, spring onions, cucumber and red pepper into 7.5cm (3in) long batons about 1cm (½in) thick. Arrange the 2 bowls with the anchovy dip on a large platter and arrange all the crudités, including the courgettes and baby corn, around them. Serve.

Spiedino di Mare Orientale

Thai Mixed Seafood and Vegetable Brochettes

This is a best-seller at Zilli Fish and one of my favourites because I love cooking with coconut. As I am based close to Chinatown, I never have any problems buying the ingredients, but I've made sure that most of those used here are available in supermarkets. Palm sugar has a delicious taste and is very different to brown sugar; however the dish won't be ruined if you can't find it. You can find galangal, which has an earthy aroma, in oriental supermarkets.

To make the brochettes, use eight 25cm (10in) bamboo skewers but soak them first in cold water to prevent the food from sticking.

SERVES 4
PREPARATION TIME: 35 MINUTES
COOKING TIME: 20 MINUTES

FOR THE COCONUT RICE
400g (14oz) long-grain rice, washed and drained
200ml (7fl oz) canned coconut milk
15ml (1 tablespoon) granulated sugar

FOR THE THAI HERB SAUCE
300ml (2 tablespoons) peanut oil
2 garlic cloves, crushed
1 fresh green chilli, seeded and finely chopped
1 stick of lemon grass, finely chopped
2.5cm (1in) piece of fresh galangal, peeled and finely chopped
200ml (7fl oz) canned coconut milk
15ml (1 teaspoon) palm sugar
juice of 1 lime

8 fresh kaffir lime leaves, shredded
300ml (10fl oz) double cream
45g (1½oz) finely chopped fresh coriander leaves
salt and freshly ground pepper

FOR THE BROCHETTES
8 red cherry tomatoes
1 medium courgette, trimmed and cut into 8 thin slices
½ medium aubergine, cut lengthways, then into 8 x 2.5cm (1in) pieces
125g (4½oz) tuna fillet
125g (4½oz) salmon fillet
125g (4½oz) monkfish fillet
125g (4½oz) swordfish fillet
125g (4½oz) red snapper fillet
8 fresh kaffir lime leaves
4 raw king prawns
25ml (1½ tablespoons) peanut oil

❍ Place the rice, coconut milk and granulated sugar in a large pan and cover with enough cold water to bring the liquid about 2.5cm (1in) above the rice. Bring to boiling point, reduce the heat, cover and simmer for 10 minutes until all the liquid has been absorbed. Remove from the heat and keep the pan covered for 10 minutes to allow the rice to steam until tender.

❍ Meanwhile, heat the oil in a saucepan, add the garlic, chilli, lemon grass and galangal and stir-fry for 2–3 minutes until soft but not brown. Stir in the coconut milk, palm sugar, lime juice and lime leaves and cook for 2 minutes. Stir in the cream and cook for 10 minutes to reduce slightly.

❍ Wrap each tomato with a courgette piece and thread 1 onto each skewer. Add an aubergine piece to each. Cut all the fish into 4 pieces and randomly thread onto the skewers, adding a lime leaf or two in between the fish. End with a prawn. Brush the brochettes with oil and season all over to taste.

❍ Pre-heat a ridged cast-iron grill pan and brush with a little oil.

❍ Place the brochettes on the grill pan and cook, turning several times, for 6–7 minutes until the fish is tender and the prawns turn pink.

❍ Meanwhile, add the coriander leaves to the sauce, season to taste and heat through for 1–2 minutes.

❍ Divide the rice among 4 large serving plates, place 2 brochettes on top, then spoon the sauce over them. Serve immediately.

Razza al Burro e Salvia

Skate with Butter and Sage

As far as I'm concerned this is the way to cook skate – quickly and simply. Sage cooked in butter gives off beautiful flavours that bring out the best in this fish. You may find that one frying pan is not large enough to hold all four skate wings, so simply use two pans and split the ingredients between each one. Skate is very inexpensive. If only large skate wings are available, just cut them into smaller pieces.
Serve this dish with a tomato, red onion and black olive salad.

SERVES 4
PREPARATION TIME: 15 MINUTES
COOKING TIME: 20 MINUTES

30ml (2 tablespoons) extra virgin olive oil
125g (4½oz) butter
8 whole fresh sage leaves

60ml (4 tablespoons) plain flour
4 x 200g (7oz) skate wings
170g (6oz) capers in brine, drained
150ml (5fl oz) dry white wine
60ml (4 tablespoons) chopped fresh flat-leaf parsley
45ml (3 tablespoons) chopped fresh sage leaves
salt and freshly ground black pepper

❍ Pre-heat the oven to 200°C/400°F/Gas Mark 6.

❍ Heat a large frying pan, add the oil and heat until hot. Add half of the butter and heat until foaming. Add the whole sage leaves and cook for 30 seconds. Remove and reserve for garnish.

❍ Spread the flour on a flat plate and season with salt and pepper. Coat the skate in the seasoned flour, shake off the excess and add to the pan. Fry for 3 minutes on each side. Transfer the skate to a baking tray and bake for 15 minutes until crisp.

❍ Meanwhile, heat the remaining butter in a saucepan, stir in the capers and wine and cook for 5 minutes. Stir in the chopped parsley and sage and cook for a further 2 minutes. Season to taste.

❍ Divide the fish among 4 warmed serving plates and spoon over the butter and sage sauce. Garnish with the whole fried sage leaves and serve immediately.

Basics

Fish Stock

Fish stocks are essential to most fish recipes that require some kind of liquid, whether to make a sauce, risotto or soup. They are much faster to make than meat stocks, requiring only 20–30 minutes cooking.

For a clear stock it is important not to boil the liquid with the flavourings. If you do end up with a cloudy stock, simply whisk some egg whites with a fork, add them to the stock, heat for 2–3 minutes, then strain through muslin.

Make stock in large batches, cool it then chill or freeze in bags of 300ml (10fl oz) quantities.

MAKES 1.5 LITRES (2¾ PINTS)
PREPARATION TIME: 10 MINUTES
COOKING TIME: 30 MINUTES

1kg (2¼lb) fish bones from white fish such as sole, monkfish or turbot
2.4 litres (4 pints) water
1 large onion, halved
1 fennel bulb, quartered
2 celery sticks, trimmed and halved
1 carrot, halved
1 leek, trimmed and quartered lengthways
8 black peppercorns
4 bay leaves
3–4 sprigs of fresh flat-leaf parsley
2 sprigs of fresh thyme

❍ Wash the fish bones, removing any traces of blood as they can make the stock bitter.

❍ Put the fish bones, water, onion, fennel, celery, carrot, leek and peppercorns in a large deep pan. Tie the bay leaves, parsley and thyme together with a little string to make a bouquet garni and add to the pan. Bring to the boil, skimming the surface frequently with a skimming spoon to remove any impurities and fat from the stock.

❍ Reduce the heat to a very gentle simmer and cook for a maximum of 30 minutes, continuing to skim the surface frequently. Try to keep the vegetables and bones from disintegrating as this will make the stock cloudy.

❍ Strain the stock through muslin and set aside to cool unless required.

Court Bouillon

This is a slightly acidic, concentrated liquid which is used for boiling or poaching, in this case fish and shellfish. The acid comes from the addition of wine or vinegar. Like stock, it only needs to be cooked for a short time, but if it does end up a bit cloudy, it doesn't really matter.

The flavours of a court bouillon can vary depending on the other flavours of the dish – for instance, you can add wild fennel or leeks.

Sometimes when you are poaching fish to go in a dish that is to be strongly flavoured by other ingredients, you can cheat and poach the fish in the liquid before it has been boiled and simmered. The court bouillon can later be used as part of the sauce in the recipe, but it needs to be strained and boiled until it is reduced.

MAKES 1 LITRE (1¾ PINTS)
PREPARATION TIME: 10 MINUTES
COOKING TIME: 20 MINUTES

1.2 litres (2 pints) water
150ml (5fl oz) dry white wine

1 medium onion, halved
1 carrot, quartered
1 stick celery, trimmed and halved
8 black peppercorns
1 bay leaf
stalks from fresh flat-leaf parsley

❍ Put all the ingredients in a large deep pan and gently bring to the boil, skimming the surface with a skimming spoon. Reduce the heat and simmer for 20 minutes.

❍ Strain the court bouillon through muslin and set aside to cool unless required.

Mayonnaise

Mayonnaise is a sauce that's perfect with plain cooked fish and also delicious with mussels. Mayonnaise is also the basis of many cold sauces for fish.

For Lemon Mayonnaise, add the finely grated lemon zest and juice of 1 lemon in addition to the juice already added.

For Garlic Mayonnaise, finely crush 3 fat garlic cloves with 10ml (2 teaspoons) salt and add to the mayonnaise with an extra 15ml (1 tablespoon) lemon juice.

MAKES 300ML (10FL OZ)
PREPARATION TIME: 15–20 MINUTES

2 medium egg yolks
5ml (1 teaspoon) smooth Dijon mustard

150ml (5fl oz) extra virgin olive oil
150ml (5fl oz) sunflower oil
juice of ½ lemon
salt and freshly ground black pepper

○ Put the egg yolks, a pinch of salt and the mustard in a bowl, then beat with a metal whisk.

○ Mix both oils in a measuring jug, then gradually add a little to the egg yolks while whisking. Continue whisking and adding the oils in a thin steady stream until all the oil is added and a thick sauce is formed.

○ Whisk in the lemon juice and season to taste (if you like you could add white pepper instead!).

Tartar Sauce

This classic fish sauce partners all fried fish. If serving a platter of poached fish and shellfish, tartar sauce is also good to have as an accompaniment.

The basis of the sauce is Mayonnaise (see page 166), to which you can add the ingredients below, or olives, lemon juice and seasonings.

Tartar sauce also makes a good accompaniment to vegetables.

MAKES 150ML (5FL OZ)
PREPARATION TIME: 10 MINUTES

150ml (5fl oz) mayonnaise (see page 166)
1 shallot, finely chopped

15ml (1 tablespoon) finely chopped fresh
flat-leaf parsley
15ml (1 tablespoon) capers, rinsed, patted dry
with kitchen paper and chopped
2 small gherkins, finely diced

❍ Mix together all the ingredients. Serve immediately, or chill, covered with cling film, in the fridge until required.

Guacamole

This is a variation on the classic Mexican avocado dip. I like to serve it with the Crab and Tropical Fruit Salad (see page 58), and it is also good with plain poached fish, or chargrilled or barbecued salmon or cod. Guacamole is a delicious and colourful addition when you are making sandwiches with fish.

To prevent the guacamole turning brown when it is chilling, reserve the stones from the avocado and place them in the dip. Remove them before serving.

MAKES 150ML (5FL OZ)
PREPARATION TIME: 10 MINUTES

2 ripe avocados
grated zest and juice of 1 lime
3 spring onions, trimmed and finely chopped

45ml (3 tablespoons) chopped fresh coriander leaves
1 fresh green chilli, seeded and finely diced
salt and freshly ground black pepper

○ Split the avocados in half and remove the stone (see page 33).

○ Peel the avocados, then roughly mash with a fork, but do not make the consistency too smooth. Add the lime zest and juice, spring onions, coriander and chilli. Stir to mix and season well to taste.

○ Chill, with the stone and covered in cling film, in the fridge until required.

Lemon Dressing

When it comes to serving fish, lemon and extra virgin olive oil take some beating. This dressing is perfect for plain cooked fish and shellfish. It can also be used as a basic marinade for barbecuing and grilling fish. It really is quite marvellous.
When I'm really lazy, I simply drizzle the cooked fish with extra virgin olive oil and balsamic vinegar – that's all it takes!

MAKES 150ML (5FL OZ)
PREPARATION TIME: 5 MINUTES PLUS
20 MINUTES STANDING
COOKING TIME: 2 MINUTES

150ml (5fl oz) extra virgin olive oil
2 fat garlic cloves, bruised with skins still on

finely grated zest of 2 lemons
1 sprig of fresh thyme
45–60ml (3–4 tablespoons) fresh lemon juice
5ml (1 teaspoon) clear honey
salt and freshly ground black pepper

❍ Put the oil, garlic, lemon zest and thyme in a heavy-based deep pan and heat until the oil is hot. Remove from the heat, cover tightly and leave for 20 minutes for the flavours to infuse.

❍ Strain the oil and add the lemon juice, honey and seasoning. Serve immediately, or store in a screw-top jar in the fridge until required.

Classic Marie-Rose Dressing

This is the classic recipe for prawn cocktail. I like to serve it as a dip with a selection of fresh shellfish.

MAKES 150ML (5FL OZ)
PREPARATION TIME: 10 MINUTES

75ml (5 tablespoons) mayonnaise (see page 166)
175ml (6fl oz) tomato ketchup

45ml (3 tablespoons) creamed horseradish sauce
15ml (1 tablespoon) freshly squeezed lemon juice

❍ Put all the ingredients in a bowl and stir to combine. Chill, covered with cling film, in the fridge until required.

Red Pepper Salsa

This is another one of my favourite dressings for fish. It appears on the menus of all my restaurants – the simple flavours bring out the best in both fish and shellfish, and the colour also helps the presentation.

If you can find organic peppers or even imported Italian or French peppers, they will be better, as they seem to have less water and a lot more flavour. I also find that they're much better roasted and peeled as they don't lose their shape. The colour of peppers can be varied, using yellow or orange, if desired.

MAKES 150ML (5FL OZ)
PREPARATION TIME: 20 MINUTES
COOKING TIME: 15–20 MINUTES

1 large red pepper
90ml (6 tablespoons) extra virgin olive oil

grated zest and juice of 1 lemon
12 fresh basil leaves
salt and freshly ground black pepper

❍ Pre-heat the oven to 200°C/400°F/Gas Mark 6.

❍ Rub the pepper with a little oil and place on a baking tray. Roast for 10–15 minutes, turning once until just browned and the skin blisters. Alternatively, the pepper can be charred on a ridged cast-iron grill pan. (Grilling on a conventional grill seems to cook peppers too much, making them too soft to peel and use in a salsa.)

❍ Allow the pepper to cool slightly, then peel the skin. Open out the pepper, catching and reserving any juices. Discard the seeds and finely slice the pepper, then dice or cut into diamond shapes. Place the pepper in the bowl with the reserved juices and stir in the remaining oil, lemon zest and juice and seasoning to taste. Tear the basil leaves and stir them into the salsa. Serve warm or cold, or store in an airtight container in the fridge for up to three days.

Basic White Pasta Dough

If you have time, it is really worth the effort making your own pasta. I just cannot explain how delicate fresh home-made pasta really is. And it is essential to use 00 flour – ordinary flour just does not work. This flour is available from most large supermarkets and all Italian delis. See specific recipes for cooking times.

SERVES 4
PREPARATION TIME: 45 MINUTES PLUS
30 MINUTES RESTING

400g (14oz) 00 flour
5 medium eggs, lightly beaten

a good pinch of salt
30ml (2 tablespoons) extra virgin olive oil
15–30ml (1–2 tablespoons) cold water
extra flour for dusting pasta

❍ Put the flour on a work surface, make a well in the centre and add the eggs, salt and oil. Moving your fingertips in a circular motion, slowly incorporate the flour into the egg mixture, adding water if required to form a dough. Knead for 5 minutes, adding extra flour to the surface, if necessary, until the dough is elastic and springs back when gently pressed. Cover with cling film and allow to rest for 30 minutes in the fridge.

❍ I recommend that you use a pasta machine for rolling out and cutting the pasta to the desired shape. If you try to roll it out with a rolling pin it will take too long and it's most unlikely that you'll roll it out thin enough.

Basic Spinach Pasta Dough

Spinach is one of the most popular ingredients used as a flavouring for fresh pasta. Called *pasta verde*, it is a classic accompaniment to egg pasta in the dish known as Hay and Straw (see page 101). See specific recipes for cooking times.

SERVES 4
PREPARATION TIME: 45 MINUTES PLUS
30 MINUTES RESTING

400 (14oz) 00 flour
2 medium eggs, plus 1 egg yolk, lightly beaten

a good pinch of salt
55g (2oz) cooked, well-drained and puréed spinach
30ml (2 tablespoons) extra virgin olive oil
15–30ml (1–2 tablespoons) cold water
extra flour for dusting pasta

❍ Put the flour on a work surface, make a well in the centre and add the eggs, salt, spinach and oil. Moving your fingertips in a circular motion, slowly incorporate the flour into the egg mixture, adding water if required to form a dough. Knead for 5 minutes, adding extra flour to the surface, if necessary, until the dough is elastic and springs back when gently pressed. Cover with cling film and allow to rest for 30 minutes in the fridge.

❍ I recommend that you use a pasta machine for rolling out and cutting the pasta to the desired shape. If you try to roll it out with a rolling pin it will take too long and it's most unlikely that you'll be able roll it out thin enough.

Gnocchi

Gnocchi can either be made with potato or semolina – in both cases they're very simple to make. Here I use potatoes. It's essential to boil them in their skins so that they don't absorb moisture when they are cooked.

The gnocchi can be made well in advance and frozen before cooking – just spread them on a large tray and freeze. Once frozen, pack in freezer bags. Cook them straight from frozen.

SERVES 4
PREPARATION TIME: 30 MINUTES
COOKING TIME: 25 MINUTES

340g (12oz) baking potatoes, scrubbed but not peeled

115g (4oz) 00 flour
a pinch of salt
55g (2oz) finely grated Parmesan cheese
3 medium egg yolks
extra flour for dusting

❍ Place the potatoes in a large pan of salted water and bring to the boil. Cook for 15–20 minutes until soft. Drain and allow to 'steam' in the pan until cool enough to handle. Peel the potatoes, then mash with a potato masher.

❍ Sprinkle the work surface with some of the measured flour, place the mashed potatoes on top and make a well in the centre. Add the remaining flour, salt, Parmesan cheese and egg yolks, slowly incorporating the ingredients together.

❍ Roll the potato mixture into a long sausage shape about 2.5cm (1in) in diameter. Dust the dough with extra flour if it starts to stick to the work surface. Cut at regular 1cm (½in) intervals.

❍ Bring a large pan of salted water to a rolling boil. Working in batches, add the half of the gnocchi to the pan and return to a rolling boil. Cook for 2–3 minutes until the gnocchi rise to the surface, then cook for a further 30 seconds until al dente. Drain and keep warm while cooking the remaining gnocchi. Serve immediately or add to a sauce.

Bruschetta

Garlic and Olive Oil Toast

Although very traditional in Italy, bruschetta seems to be the garlic bread of the 1990s.
Delicious rustic country bread toasted, rubbed with garlic and served with soups,
salads, hot pots ... in fact anything that has lots of juices to mop up.
Bruschette are also served in their own glory topped with a selection of Italian
specialities such as sun-dried tomatoes in oil, Parma ham, mozzarella, dolcelatte ...
the list is endless!
To make bruschetta, choose from the wonderful selection of Italian breads now
available in supermarkets, bakeries and delis. Opt for a bread such as puglia or
ciabatta; the bread must not be too heavy.

SERVES 4
PREPARATION TIME: 5 MINUTES PLUS
10–15 MINUTES STANDING
COOKING TIME: 4 MINUTES

1 round or long loaf of Italian country bread
4 garlic cloves, halved

150ml (5fl oz) extra virgin olive oil
salt and freshly ground black pepper

❍ Pre-heat a ridged cast-iron grill pan on the hob until smoking.

❍ While the grill pan is heating, cut the bread into 2.5cm (1in) thick slices.

❍ Toast the bread slices on the grill pan for about 2 minutes on each side. Rub the toast with the garlic and place on a large platter.

❍ Drizzle the toast with half of the oil, breaking the surface a little to allow the oil to soak through. Season to taste. Turn the toast over and drizzle with the remaining oil. Allow the toast to sit in the oil for 10–15 minutes before serving.

Cook's Notes

Weights and Measures

British cooks generally measure liquids by volume and solids by weight, whereas American and Australian cooks measure both liquids and many solid ingredients by volume. The following chart gives approximate equivalent metric, imperial and standard spoon and cup measures used in this book – they have been adjusted slightly up or down to make them more usable. Note that the American pint contains 16fl oz, whereas a British/Australian pint is 20fl oz. British cooks should follow all metric or all imperial measurements in the recipes – these measurements are not interchangeable.

LIQUID MEASURES

METRIC	IMPERIAL	STANDARD SPOON/CUP MEASURE
30ml	1fl oz	2 tablespoons
60ml	2fl oz	4 tablespoons or ¼ cup
75ml	2½fl oz	5 tablespoons
80ml	2¾fl oz	⅓ cup
90ml	3fl oz	
120m	4fl oz	½ cup
150ml	5fl oz	
175ml	6fl oz	¾ cup
200ml	7fl oz	
240ml	8fl oz	1 cup (½ US pint)
275ml	9fl oz	
300ml	10fl oz (½ pint)	1¼ cups
360ml	12fl oz	1½ cups
400ml	14fl oz	1¾ cups
450ml	15fl oz	
500ml	16fl oz	2 cups (1 US pint)
600ml	1 pint	2½ cups
750ml	1¼ pints	3 cups
900ml	1½ pints	3½ cups
1 litre	1¾ pints	4 cups (1 US quart)
1.5 litres	2¾ pints	6 cups (1½ US quarts)

STANDARD SPOON MEASURES

When measuring in spoons, always use standard metric measuring spoons with the ingredients levelled. The difference between standard metric and standard American measuring spoons is negligible. The Australian standard tablespoon, however, which is equivalent to 4 standard teaspoons, holds 20ml.

SPOON MEASURE	UK METRIC	AUSTRALIAN METRIC
¼ teaspoon	1.25ml	1.25ml
½ teaspoon	2.5ml	2.5ml
1 teaspoon	5ml	5ml
1 tablespoon	15ml	20ml

STANDARD CUP MEASURES

It's impossible to give a single standard cup weight for all dry ingredients because the same volume of one ingredient will weigh a different amount from the same volume of another. Some of the more common ingredients traditionally measured by cup in the US and/or Australia are listed below; these ingredients appear in this book.

1 CUP OF	APPROX WEIGHT EQUIVALENT
butter (2 US sticks)	225g (8oz)
freshly grated Parmesan cheese	115g (4oz)
cream (single, double)	240ml (8fl oz)
white flour*	115g (4oz)
white granulated/caster sugar	200g (7oz)
dry breadcrumbs	115g (4oz)
fresh breadcrumbs	55g (2oz)
small pasta shapes	115g (4oz)
chopped onion	140g (5oz)
chopped pepper	115g (4oz)
chopped tomatoes	225g (8oz)
diced aubergine	115g (4oz)
diced raw potato	150g (5½oz)
mashed potato	115g (4oz)
shelled peas	115g (4oz)
sliced mushrooms	85g (3oz)

* American all-purpose flour is milled from a mixture of hard and soft wheats, whereas British plain flour is made mainly from soft wheat. Although 1 cup of British flour weighs approximately 115g (4oz), the American equivalent cup weight of all-purpose flour will weigh 140g (5oz). The flour should be adjusted accordingly. The Italian soft wheat 00 flour used for making pasta is available in delis and large supermarkets; all readers should use the quantity specified in the recipe.

Glossary

Although the enjoyment of food is common to all nations, the names by which we know even the most basic ingredients can vary. The following list gives UK, US and Australian terminology for ingredients used in this book.

UK	US	AUSTRALIA
Dairy Products		
single cream	light cream	single cream
double cream	heavy cream	heavy cream
egg: med (53–63g)	large egg (56g)	egg:med (53–63g)
egg: large (63–73g)*	extra large egg (63g)	egg: large (63–73g)
pecorino cheese	Romano cheese	Romano cheese

*Eggs are assumed to be large in these recipes unless otherwise indicated.

UK	US	AUSTRALIA
Dry Ingredients, Nuts and Storecupboard Items		
cornflour	cornstarch	cornflour
granulated sugar	granulated sugar	white crystal sugar
pine nuts	pignoli/pine nuts	pine nuts
plain flour	all-purpose flour	plain flour
tomato purée	tomato paste	tomato purée

UK	US	AUSTRALIA
Vegetables and Herbs		
aubergine	eggplant	aubergine
celeriac	celery root/celeriac	celeriac
chick pea	garbanzo bean/chick pea	chick pea
chicory	Belgian endive	witloof/chicory
chips	French fries	chips
coriander (fresh)	cilantro	coriander (fresh)
courgettes	zucchini	courgettes
endive/frisée	curly endive	endive/frisée
fennel	fennel/finocchio	fennel
mooli	daikon	mooli
pepper	sweet/bell pepper	capsicum
rocket	arugula	rocket
spinach	spinach	English spinach
spring onion	scallion/green onion	spring onion
sweetcorn	corn	sweetcorn
sweet potato	orange-fleshed sweet potato (not yam)	orange sweet potato

UK	US	AUSTRALIA
Fish and Shellfish		
cod	cod, Pacific cod	blue cod
Dover sole	English sole	sole
John Dory	John Dory, Oreo Dory	John Dory
lemon sole	English sole	sole
monkfish	monkfish, anglerfish	monkfish
prawns	shrimp or prawns**	prawns
king prawns	jumbo shrimp	king prawns
scallops	sea, bay scallops	sea, bay scallops
shrimp	baby/cocktail shrimp	shrimp
squid	squid, calamari	squid, calamari

** In some parts of the US, the term prawn is used for very large shrimp, but in general, shrimp (small, medium, large, jumbo) is the American terminology. Note that Dublin bay prawns, langoustines and scampi belong to the same family as lobster.

UK	US	AUSTRALIA
Cookware and Paper Products		
baking tray	baking sheet	baking tray
frying pan	skillet	frying pan
grill***	broiler	griller
ridged cast-iron grill pan	range-top grill	griddle
roasting tin	roasting pan	roasting tin
fish slice	slotted spatula	fish slice
cling film	plastic wrap	cling film
greaseproof paper	waxed paper	greaseproof paper
kitchen paper	paper towels	absorbent paper
tea towel	dish towel	tea towel
muslin	cheesecloth	muslin
wooden cocktail stick	toothpick	toothpick

***British and Australian cooks grill whereas Americans broil, except for barbecued food, which is grilled in all three countries.

Index

If you enjoyed this book then you will love
Zilli's Italian Food for Friends – an amazing selection
of simple and mouthwatering Italian recipes.

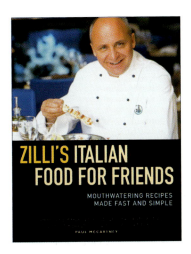

Available from all good bookshops,
or by mail order from 020 7381 0666.